39270

FURTHER TOUGHER CLOSER VOLVO OCEAN RACE

39270

FURTHER TOUGHER CLOSER VOLVO OCEAN RACE

First published in 2012
© **Volvo Ocean Race, S.L.U.**

Volvo Ocean Race, S.L.U.
Muelle Nº 10 de Levante
Puerto de Alicante
03001 Alicante, SPAIN
Email: info@volvooceanrace.com
Fax: +34 966 080 389

volvooceanrace.com

Endeavour London Ltd.
21–31 Woodfield Road
London W9 2BA, UNITED KINGDOM
info@endeavourlondon.com

ISBN 978-1-908271-82-2

Published in France by Solar Editions
ISBN 978-2-263-06140-0

A catalogue record for this book is available
from the British Library.

Publisher
Volvo Ocean Race, S.L.U.

Concept
Crescendo Brands & Designers United
Project Director
Gavin Brown
Creative Directors
Dimitris Koliadimas, Dimitris Papazoglou
Layout and Design
Dimitris Koliadimas, Vassiliki Argyropoulou, Eleftheria Straka
Author
Gavin Brown
Translators
Agathe Armand, Miriam Torres Brinkmann, George Zhao
Editorial Advisors
Kevin Fylan & Tim Stonton, Volvo Ocean Race, S.L.U.
Production Advisors
Charles Merullo & Mary Osborne, Endeavour London Ltd.

Printed in Italy by Arti Grafiche Johnson S.p.A.
Typeset in Forza font family & printed on Arctic Ivory paper.

Volvo Ocean Race, Volvo Group and **Volvo Car Corporation**
would like to extend warm thanks to the family of sponsors for their vital
contribution to the success of the Volvo Ocean Race 2011-12:
Inmarsat
The Boston Consulting Group
Abu Dhabi Tourism & Culture Authority
DHL
Thrane & Thrane
IWC Schaffhausen
PUMA
Volvo Penta
Ericsson
Volvo IT

Navigation
Volvo Ocean Race
2011-12

Cumulative
Distance (nm)

Teams

Abu Dhabi Ocean Racing
UAE

Ian Walker GBR

Nick Dana USA
Justin Ferris NZL
Simon Fisher GBR
Rob Greenhalgh GBR
Adil Khalid UAE
Andrew Lewis USA
Wade Morgan AUS
Anthony Nossiter AUS
Jules Salter GBR
Craig Satterthwaite NZL
Justin Slattery IRL
Paul Willcox RSA

CAMPER with Emirates
Team New Zealand ESP/NZL

Chris Nicholson AUS

Stu Bannatyne NZL
'Chuny' Bermúdez ESP
Nick Burridge NZL
Hamish Hooper NZL
Andrew McLean NZL
Adam Minoprio NZL
Will Oxley AUS
Mike Pammenter RSA
Tony Rae NZL
Rob Salthouse NZL
Daryl Wislang NZL

Groupama sailing team
FRA

Franck Cammas FRA

Charles Caudrelier FRA
Thomas Coville FRA
Damian Foxall IRL
Phil Harmer AUS
Erwan Israël FRA
Martin Krite SWE
Brad Marsh NZL
Jean-Luc Nélias FRA
Laurent Pagès FRA
Yann Riou FRA
Martin Strömberg SWE

PUMA Ocean Racing powered by BERG USA

Ken Read USA

Tom Addis AUS
Shannon Falcone ANT
Ryan Godfrey AUS
Kelvin Harrap NZL
Brad Jackson NZL
Thomas Johanson FIN
Rome Kirby USA
Michi Müller GER
Tony Mutter NZL
Amory Ross USA
Casey Smith AUS
Jono Swain RSA

Team Sanya CHN

Mike Sanderson NZL

Cameron Dunn NZL
Jared Henderson NZL
Ryan Houston NZL
Teng Jiang He 'Tiger' CHN
Martin Kirketerp DEN
Aksel Magdahl NOR
Chris Main NZL
Richard Mason NZL
Andy Meiklejohn NZL
David Rolfe NZL
Bert Schandevyl BEL
Andrés Soriano ESP
Dave Swete NZL

Team Telefónica ESP

Iker Martínez ESP

Pablo Arrarte ESP
Jordi Calafat ESP
Andrew Cape AUS
'Ñeti' Cuervas-Mons ESP
Xabi Fernández ESP
Diego Fructuoso ESP
Zane Gills AUS
Iñigo Losada ESP
Neal McDonald GBR
Pepe Ribes ESP
'Joca' Signorini BRA

Official Route

Alicante

Abu Dhabi

Sanya

Cape Town

Auckland

Galway

Lorient

Lisbon

Miami

Itajaí

ALICANTE

14 Oct – 5 Nov 2011
Iberdrola In-Port Race: *29 Oct 2011, 13:00 UTC*
Leg 1 Start: *5 Nov 2011, 13:00 UTC*
Official Distance: *6,500 nm*

The first 6,500 nautical miles of the Volvo Ocean Race 2011-12 promised more than just the opening page of ocean racing's greatest epic. Important clues to the shape of the entire contest lay ahead. Ever since the race went single class in 1997-98, the winner of the first leg had gone on to take overall victory, making the long slog south from Alicante to Cape Town a vital touchstone.

Five of the six teams that lined up on Spain's Costa Blanca for the opening leg in November 2011 could justifiably dream of glory in Galway, with Team Sanya the only real outsiders in their older generation boat. To the experts dockside, the race would come down to nuances.

If that's what logic told us, it forgot to tell Nature. Nuances were brushed aside as Leg 1 was defined by extremes from the very start. The toughest racetrack in world sport wasted no time in reminding us of its power. Even the Mediterranean seemed determined to treat the teams' meticulous preparation with contempt.

On land too, the race demanded a high price of shore crews, Race Control staff, logistics teams and media as they scrambled to respond to the events playing out on the water. Friends and families of the sailors knew they would not be able to rest easy until the teams arrived safely in Galway.

It was exhilarating and terrifying all at once. Life At The Extreme was back in fashion and would become a consuming obsession for all the sailors – and the rest of us – for the next eight months.

CAPE TOWN

KEN READ / PUMA, PRINCE CARL PHILIP OF SWEDEN

FERNANDO TORRES, SERGIO BUSQUETS

The race's patron takes a front-row seat aboard PUMA for the opening in-port race.

Siège au premier plan pour le parrain de la course lors de l'in-port d'ouverture, à bord de PUMA.

El patrono oficial de la regata en primera fila de la in-port a bordo del PUMA.

瑞典王子卡尔·菲利普在首场港内赛中登上彪马队赛船。

In Alicante for a Euro 2012 qualifier, football's world champions tour the race village.

À Alicante pour la qualification de l'Euro 2012, les champions du monde de football visitent le village.

En Alicante para un encuentro clasificatorio para la Eurocopa 2012, los campeones del mundo visitan el village.

世界杯冠军西班牙足球队在阿利坎特参加欧洲杯预选赛期间造访赛事村。

MIKE SANDERSON / TEAM SANYA, PRINCESS LETIZIA OF SPAIN

KNUT FROSTAD, VOLVO OCEAN RACE ACADEMY

The Godmother to Team Telefónica's boat meets the teams.

La parraine de Team Telefónica rencontre les équipages.

La madrina del barco Telefónica conoce a los equipos.

西班牙王妃莱斯奇亚与各船队见面。

The Race CEO gives local youth sailors a tour of the control room at Race Headquarters.

Le directeur de la course fait visiter la salle de contrôle du quartier général aux jeunes régatiers locaux.

El Director General de la regata enseña la sala de control del Cuartel General a unos niños alicantinos.

赛事首席执行官带领当地儿童参观比赛总控室。

2011-12 RACE FLEET, VISITOR PAVILIONS

Recalling the spirit of 2008, Alicante's party mood fuels the start port atmosphere.

Dans l'esprit de 2008, l'ambiance festive d'Alicante nourrit l'atmosphère du port de départ.

Rememorando el espíritu de 2008, la atmósfera festiva en Alicante caldea el ambiente de la salida.

就像2008年的启航一样，阿利坎特让赛事启航充满狂欢气氛。

IAN WALKER, SIMON FISHER / ABU DHABI OCEAN RACING, ZINEDINE ZIDANE

The football legend prepares to jump from Azzam at the start of Leg 1.

Le légendaire footballer se prépare à sauter d'Azzam pour le départ de l'étape 1.

La leyenda del fútbol se prepara para saltar desde el Azzam en la salida de la Etapa 1.

足坛名将齐达内准备在第一赛段启航之际从"阿萨姆号"跳下。

STEINLAGER 2

Sir Peter Blake's 1989-90 race-winner in Alicante for the Legends regatta and race start.

Le bateau vainqueur de Sir Peter Blake en 1989-90 à Alicante pour les Legends et le départ de la course.

El ganador de la edición 1989-90 de Sir Peter Blake estuvo en Alicante para la Legends Regatta y la salida.

1989—90赛事冠军队船长彼得·布莱克爵士在阿利坎特出席传奇赛和启航。

RAMÓN CARLIN, LIONEL PÉAN, SAYULA II CREW

The winning skippers from 1973-74 and 1985-86 are among more than 600 Legends revellers.

Les skippers vainqueurs en 1973-74 et 1985-86 sont parmi les plus de 600 invités des Legends.

Los patrones ganadores de las ediciones de 1973-74 y 1985-86 están entre los más de 600 juerguistas de la Legend.

1973-74和1985-86届赛事冠军队船长和其他六百多名老船员齐聚阿利坎特。

Determined to improve on their
2008-09 placings, Team Telefónica
and PUMA Ocean Racing powered
by BERG headed a fleet packed with
champion sailors.

Déterminés à améliorer leurs résultats
de 2008-09, PUMA Ocean Racing
powered by BERG et Team Telefónica
mènent une flotte de champions.

Con el propósito de mejorar sus
posiciones de podio en la regata de
2008-09, el Telefónica y el PUMA
encabezaron una flota abarrotada de
campeones.

为了突破2008－09届比赛的名次，铆足
劲的彪马队和西班牙电信队在各支实力强
大的队伍中突出重围。

After two previous races sailed in Volvo Open 70s, the class stood uncontested as the most exciting ocean racing design ever. With the class now mature and new limits imposed on teams' ability to spend their way to success, victory in 2011-12 would – more than ever – be built on the all-round performance of boat and crew.

Against this backdrop, Abu Dhabi Ocean Racing and China's Team Sanya felt encouraged to try their hand at ocean racing's greatest test. From the island of Mallorca, CAMPER found a way to shortcut the learning curve by enlisting the expertise of Emirates Team New Zealand for a tilt at glory.

As the six teams assembled in October, each knew that the outcome of the race would be determined by their ability to respond to unforeseen events and their willingness to take calculated risks. Judgment and boat handling would be key. Above all, this was a race that would demand consistent performance in the most extreme physical and psychological conditions.

Alicante provided the stage for the first of 10 in-port races and the launch point for nine ocean legs that would put all of these qualities to the ultimate test.

Après deux éditions, les Volvo Open 70 se sont imposés comme les plus excitants des bateaux de course hauturiers. De nouvelles limites ont été fixées pour freiner les dépenses des équipes et la classe est arrivée à maturité. Plus que jamais, la victoire dépend des performances globales des bateaux et des équipages.

C'est dans ce contexte qu'Abu Dhabi Ocean Racing et Team Sanya ont décidé de participer à cette grande course au large. Depuis l'île de Majorque, CAMPER s'est associé aux experts d'Emirates Team New Zealand pour abréger son apprentissage et tenter d'atteindre la gloire.

Les six équipages se réunissent en octobre. Chacun sait alors que l'issue de la course dépend de sa connaissance du bateau, de sa gestion du risque et de sa capacité à réagir à l'imprévisible. Et par dessus tout, de performances régulières dans les conditions les plus extrêmes physiquement et psychologiquement.

Point de départ des neuf étapes de large qui mettront ces qualités à l'épreuve, Alicante accueille aussi la première des 10 courses in-port.

Con dos ediciones en su haber, los Volvo Open 70 no han encontrado rival como los barcos de regatas de altura más emocionantes de la historia. Ahora que son maduros como clase, la victoria sería el resultado -más que nunca- del rendimiento del barco y la tripulación. Además, las nuevas reglas limitaron los gastos de los equipos.

En este contexto, equipos como el Abu Dhabi Ocean Racing y el Team Sanya sintieron que podían intentar ganar el mayor premio de las regatas oceánicas. Desde Mallorca, CAMPER encontró un atajo en la curva de aprendizaje al fichar al Emirates Team New Zealand –la escuadra que lleva años en la élite de la vela– para su asalto a la gloria.

Cuando los seis equipos se juntaron en octubre, todos sabían que el resultado de la regata lo decidiría el conocimiento del barco, la preparación para asumir riesgos calculados y la capacidad de respuesta ante lo desconocido. Sobre todo, la clave estaría en un rendimiento consistente en las condiciones físicas y psicológicas más extremas.

Alicante ofreció el escenario de la primera de diez pruebas in-port y el comienzo de nueve etapas oceánicas que iban a poner a prueba todas estas cualidades.

沃尔沃Open70大帆船已是第三次现身沃尔沃环球帆船赛，各项性能日渐成熟，想要赢得比赛要求赛船和船队拥有比以往更出色的表现，而新的比赛规则也让船队的夺冠之路充满限制。

在这样的大背景下，来自阿布扎比和中国的"阿萨姆号"和"三亚号"跃跃欲试，成为赛事近四十年历史中第一批来自亚洲的比赛队伍。

来自西班牙马洛卡的企业看步与著名的西班牙酋长队联合组队，直指冠军头衔。

当六支队伍十月齐聚，每支船队都深知，比赛的结局将和船员对船只的了解程度、保守与冒险的平衡、应对突发情况的能力等因素密切相关，更重要的是在极端的体能和心理条件下持续稳定的发挥。

阿利坎特的港内赛是十场港内赛中的第一场，也开启了环绕地球的九个赛段的争夺，各队的实力将在接下来的比赛中充分展现。

Groupama were the first French race entrants since 1993-94. The hopes of an ocean racing-mad nation rested on the shoulders of the prolific Franck Cammas.

Groupama est le premier concurrent français depuis 1993. Tous les espoirs d'un pays fou de course au large reposent sur les épaules du prodige Franck Cammas.

El Groupama fue el primer equipo francés desde 1993-94. Las esperanzas de una nación apasionada por las regatas de altura descansaban sobre los hombros del prodigioso Frank Cammas.

安盟保险队是1993年以来赛事的第一支法国船队，这个航海大国将厚望都寄托在了极具耐力的船长弗兰科·卡玛斯身上。

The joy of Azzam's commanding in-port race win was shattered along with her mast on the first night of Leg 1. For Abu Dhabi, on debut, it was a sober initiation to the race.

La joie d'Azzam, vainqueur de l'in-port, se brise avec son mât lors de la première nuit de l'étape 1. Un début de course qui leur donne à réfléchir.

La alegría del Azzam por su victoria en la regata in-port se hizo trizas junto con su mástil en la primera noche de la Etapa 1. Para los debutantes, fue el más triste de los comienzos.

"阿萨姆号"赢得港内赛的喜悦被第一赛段第一天比赛中桅杆折断的事故击碎，对于初次亮相的船队，这一天永远无法忘记。

Still on Day 1, a deep gash opened
in Sanya's bow, abruptly ending the
underdog's leg. Only watertight doors
below deck prevented a catastrophe.

Jour 1 toujours : une large fissure
s'ouvre sur l'étrave de Sanya, mettant
fin à l'étape de l'outsider. Seules
les portes étanches empêchent la
catastrophe.

El primer día se abrió una profunda
brecha en la proa del Sanya, que
terminó abruptamente con su etapa.
Los mamparos estancos previnieron
una catástrofe.

同样是比赛第一天，"三亚号"船头被划
开一道大大的伤口，导致船队直接退出第
一赛段，船舱内的水密门避免了一场更大
事故的发生。

The first 24 hours had dealt the fleet a brutal hand. Now, two teams faced enormous odds just to get back in the race.

Les 24 premières heures ont malmené la flotte. Deux équipes font désormais face à un vrai défi pour revenir dans la course.

Las primeras 24 horas fueron devastadoras. Ahora, dos equipos tenían pocas posibilidades de reincorporarse a la regata.

头24小时让各支队伍深感压力，而两支出现事故的船队现在要排除万难，尽早返赛。

As the remaining fleet headed out into the Atlantic, Franck Cammas' Groupama gambled on hugging the African coast to build advantage.

Pendant que le reste de la flotte s'éloigne en Atlantique, le Groupama de Franck Cammas fait le pari de coller à la côte africaine pour prendre l'avantage.

Mientras lo que queda de flota se adentra en el Atlántico, el Groupama de Franck Cammas se la jugó a rodear la costa de África para ganar ventaja.

在其他队伍一路向西进入大西洋之际，弗兰科·卡玛斯率领的安盟保险队决定赌一把，沿着非洲大陆南下。

Boldness turned to burden as Groupama's handy lead became a punishing deficit. They would never recover the miles lost on the leg.

Leur audace ne paye pas et l'avance de Groupama se transforme en un retard cuisant. Ils ne récupéreront pas les milles perdus.

La audacia se les convirtió en lastre y su liderato inicial se tornó en una desventaja de la que ya nunca se recuperarían.

安盟保险队逐渐失掉城池，并且难以再次挽回。

Strike three. Chasing Telefónica hard, Mar Mostro's mast came crashing down. PUMA's hopes of challenging for victory in Cape Town were in tatters.

Troisième crise. En pourchassant Telefónica, le mât de Mar Mostro tombe. Plus d'espoir de scorer au Cap pour PUMA.

Tercera caída en combate. Persiguiendo al Telefónica, el Mar Mostro desarboló. Las esperanzas del PUMA de obtener un buen resultado hechas jirones.

第三起事故发生了。在努力追赶西班牙电信队时，彪马队桅杆发生断裂。彪马队想要率先抵达开普敦的愿望被残酷的现实击碎。

"This is the saddest and most disappointed 11 people on earth," said Ken Read, reflecting on the mammoth task now confronting his team.

« Voilà les 11 personnes les plus tristes et les plus déçues sur terre, » confie alors Ken Read devant le nouveau challenge qui attend son équipe.

"Somos las once personas más tristes y decepcionadas del mundo," reflexionaba Ken Read sobre la cuesta arriba a la que se enfrentaba ahora su equipo.

"这是这个地球上最伤心和失落的11个人"，肯·里德谈及船队事故时说。

With PUMA out, CAMPER had five days to close down Telefónica's lead. High speeds dominated the final 2,000 nm to Cape Town.

PUMA parti, CAMPER a cinq jours pour reprendre l'avance de Telefónica. Les derniers 2000 milles avant Le Cap se font à haute vitesse.

Con el PUMA fuera, el CAMPER tenía cinco días para alcanzar al Telefónica. Las altas velocidades dominaron las últimas 2000 millas náuticas hasta Ciudad del Cabo.

看步·新西兰酋长队在第一赛段中创造的24小时航行553海里的速度纪录直到比赛快要结束时才被超越。

Pushing boat and bodies to the limit, CAMPER's blistering 24-hour run of 553 nm set a benchmark that would stand until late in the race.

En poussant le bateau et les corps à la limite, CAMPER parcourt 553 milles en 24 heures – une référence qui tiendra jusque tard dans la course.

Las 553 millas náuticas que el CAMPER recorrió en 24 horas llevando el barco y la tripulación al límite marcaron un hito que duraría parte de la regata.

看步·新西兰酋长队在第一赛段中创造的24小时航行533海里的速度纪录直到比赛末尾才被超越。

A flawless display of sailing saw
Telefónica to victory and marked
Iker Martínez's men out as leading
contenders for overall race honours.

Après une démonstration nautique
impeccable, Telefónica s'impose
comme un prétendant sérieux à la
victoire finale.

Un despliegue de navegación perfecta
llevó al Telefónica a la victoria y marcó
a los hombres de Iker Martínez como
favoritos para la victoria de la general.

西班牙电信队的完美表现让他们成功夺得
了赛段冠军，也让伊克尔·马丁内兹率领
的这支船队成为总冠军的最大热门。

The Spanish team's emphatic leg victory gave the race's high profile newcomer, Franck Cammas, much to contemplate.

L'emblématique victoire espagnole donne à penser à Franck Cammas, bizuth qualifié.

La contundente victoria del equipo español le dio al prominente novato, Franck Cammas, mucho en que pensar.

西班牙船队的"开门红"让首次征战沃尔沃环球帆船赛的弗兰科·卡玛斯不得不好好总结和思考。

CAPE TOWN

25 Nov 2011 – 11 Dec 2011
V&A Waterfront In-Port Race: *10 Dec 2011, 13:00 UTC*
Leg 2 Start: *11 Dec 2011, 13:00 UTC*
Official Distance: *5,430 nm*

Throughout its long history, the race has known many types of danger but the route for 2011-12 presented a whole new set of hazards. A total of 237 attacks, kidnappings and other incidents off the East African coast in 2011 meant that piracy would be the number one danger confronting the fleet in the weeks that lay ahead.

Ensuring the crews' safety in the Indian Ocean, long before reaching Abu Dhabi, would ultimately demand the most complex logistical operation ever undertaken by the race.

Cape Town – playing host to the race for a record eighth time – bid farewell to the fleet as it embarked on a 5,430 nm leg that was broken into two points-scoring stages.

Information on the fleet's approach to the Stage 1 finish line was to be kept secret. In the media blackout conditions of the 'stealth zone', Telefónica engaged with CAMPER in an almighty tussle for the lion's share of the leg points.

Once in the safe haven port, the boats were loaded onto a heavy lift ship for transit to a position off the coast of Sharjah in the northern Emirates. A final 98 nm sprint to the sparkling waters and warm welcome of Abu Dhabi remained to finish a leg that demanded a great deal from the teams, on water and on land.

A meticulously planned operation had averted a serious threat to the athletes and their boats, while giving race-watchers a graphic reminder of the grave risks sailors face.

ABU DHABI

The breakages on Leg 1 left the shore teams working frantically to ready their boats for action in Cape Town.

Les avaries de l'étape 1 contraignent les équipes techniques à un travail frénétique pour préparer les bateaux au Cap.

La carnicería de la Etapa 1 supuso que los equipos de tierra trabajaran a contrarreloj para tener listos los barcos para la acción en Ciudad del Cabo.

第一赛段的波折让岸队承受不小的压力，他们必须确保船只别来无恙，并能够在开普敦港内赛中一较高下。

Frenzied logistics and repair work meant little rest as Abu Dhabi, Sanya, and PUMA hitched rides to rejoin the race.

Logistique et travaux de réparation accordent peu de repos à Abu Dhabi, Sanya et PUMA, des équipes dont le retour dans la course est compliqué.

Frenética logística y reparaciones para que el Abu Dhabi, el Sanya, y el PUMA estuvieran listos para incorporarse a la regata.

巨大的维修和运输工作让阿布扎比队、三亚队和彪马队没有喘息的机会，立刻投入新的战斗。

Telefónica made it a clean sweep in
Cape Town, taking maximum points in
the V&A Waterfront In-Port Race.

Telefónica fait le ménage au Cap en
prenant le maximum de points dans la
course In-Port V&A Waterfront.

El Telefónica arrasa en Ciudad del
Cabo y suma el máximo número de
puntos en la regata in-port frente al
V&A Waterfront.

西班牙电信队再次称霸，在开普敦的港内
赛中全取六个积分。

Idyllic conditions and breathtaking scenery provided a frame for picture-perfect sailing.

Conditions idéales et paysage à couper le souffle offrent un cadre parfait pour naviguer.

Condiciones idílicas y un impresionante escenario para una navegación de postal.

美丽的自然风光为帆船比赛设立了如画般的大背景。

CAPE TOWN RACE VILLAGE

An excited Cape Town crowd gathers to see off the fleet.

Au Cap, un public enthousiaste se rassemble pour saluer la flotte.

El público de Ciudad del Cabo se despide de la flota.

热情的开普敦观众为船队送行。

BRYAN HABANA

The explosive rugby star gives the grinding challenge a workout.

L'explosive star du rugby s'essaye au challenge du moulin à café.

El fornido jugador de rugby practica en el simulador del grinder.

橄榄球明星在绞盘挑战器上一试身手。

NICK DANA / ABU DHABI OCEAN RACING

Azzam's Media Crew Member enjoys the Cape Town surf.

L'équipier média d'Azzam profite du surf au Cap.

El tripulante de medios del Azzam disfruta de las olas en Ciudad del Cabo.

阿布扎比队媒体船员享受在开普敦的冲浪时光。

CREW / PUMA OCEAN RACING POWERED BY BERG

Bafana Bafana! Ken Read's boys charm the local crowds.

Bafana Bafana ! Les gars de Ken Read séduisent les locaux.

¡Bafana Bafana! Los chicos de Ken Read encandilan a la afición local.

彪马队船员在开普敦当地受到追捧。

PUMA PAVILION, CAPE TOWN SHORE BASE

Defiant fans rally behind PUMA's efforts to get back in the race.	Des fans tenaces s'associent aux efforts de PUMA pour revenir dans la course.	Los aficionados apoyando los esfuerzos del PUMA de volver a la regata.	彪马队的粉丝为遭遇不测的船队加油打气。

SOFIA HELLQVIST

Project Playground children take part in a Keep the Oceans Clean! workshop.	Des enfants du Project Playground participent aux ateliers de Keep the Oceans Clean.	Niños del Projecto Playground toman parte en un taller de Keep the Oceans Clean.	小朋友参加"保持海洋清洁"为主题的艺术工作坊。

CREW / TEAM SANYA

The 669 metre Lion's Head peak provides a stunning training run location.	Les 669 mètres du sommet du Lion's Head, saisissant lieu de jogging.	La montaña Cabeza de León, de 669 metros, es perfecta para hacer ejercicio.	海拔669米的狮头山成为船员体能训练的新场所。

3D CINEMA, VOLVO OCEAN RACE EXPERIENCE

Local youth centre children enjoy one of the village's most popular attractions.	Le centre de la jeunesse locale profite d'une des animations les plus populaires du village.	El centro juvenil local disfruta de una de las muchas atracciones populares del village.	当地的青年活动中心在赛事村里颇受欢迎。

Unusually calm conditions accompanied the fleet out of Cape Town. For a week, progress for all the teams was painstaking.

Une fois partie du Cap, la flotte avance lentement pendant une semaine, dans des conditions inhabituellement calmes.

Una inusual calma acompañó a la flota en la salida de Ciudad del Cabo. Durante una semana, los equipos avanzaron a una lentitud desesperante.

微弱的海风伴随船队离开开普敦，这样的天气状况使得第一周的比赛进展缓慢。

The Chinese team surprised the fleet, heading north into torrid winds. Sanya's bold tactics looked at first to have paid off, before cruel luck again brought their leg to an abrupt end.

L'équipe chinoise surprend en partant au nord vers des vents très forts. L'audacieuse tactique de Sanya paye un temps, avant que la malchance ne mette fin à leur étape.

El equipo chino sorprendió a la flota al dirigirse al norte hacia tórridos vientos. La atrevida táctica del Sanya les benefició al principio, antes de que la cruel mala suerte pusiera un abrupto fin a su etapa.

背水一战的"三亚号"选择北上进入风暴区，一开始还高歌猛进，却不料再次遭遇不测，被迫停靠马达加斯加岛。

In the darkness of night and the
stealth zone, Telefónica edged out
CAMPER by 117 seconds to claim a
thrilling victory on the first stage of
Leg 2.

Dans la nuit et en pleine zone furtive,
Telefónica devance CAMPER de 117
secondes et remporte la première
partie de l'étape 2.

En plena noche y en modo invisible,
el Telefónica superó al CAMPER por
117 segundos, adjudicándose así
la victoria en la primera parte de la
Etapa 2.

在一片漆黑的隐密区内，西班牙电信队以
117秒的优势战胜看步·新西兰酋长队，
赢得第二赛段第一阶段比赛的胜利。

Once in the secret safe haven port, the
boats were loaded one-by-one aboard
the Happy Diamond for passage to
Sharjah.

Une fois dans le port secret, les
bateaux sont chargés un à un à bord
de l'Happy Diamond pour partir à
Sharjah.

Una vez en el puerto seguro y secreto,
se cargaron los barcos uno a uno
a bordo del Happy Diamond para
llevarlos hasta Sharjah.

抵达安全保密港后，船只被纷纷载上"欢
乐钻石号"货轮，等待运往沙迦。

Groupama showed their first glimpses of real pace by chasing down Telefónica on the sprint stage into Abu Dhabi. Victory came after last-minute repairs to a crack in her hull.

Groupama commence à révéler sa vraie vitesse en dépassant Telefónica lors du sprint vers Abu Dhabi. Une victoire qui vient après une réparation de dernière minute sur une fissure de leur coque.

El Groupama mostró los primero atisbos de auténtica velocidad en la persecución al Telefónica en el esprin hasta Abu Dabi. La victoria llegó tras una reparación de último minuto en el casco.

尽管在比赛结束前刚刚修好船身的裂痕，安盟保险队还是在向阿布扎比的冲刺中赶上了西班牙电信队。

ABU DHABI

31 Dec 2011 – 14 Jan 2012
Etihad Airways In-Port Race: *13 Jan 2012, 10:00 UTC*
Leg 3 Start: *14 Jan 2012, 10:00 UTC*
Official Distance: *4,600 nm*

'Travellers Welcome.' Never was the Abu Dhabi refrain more fitting. It was the warmest of receptions that heralded the race's first foray into Arabic waters. January 4, 2012 signaled the moment when ocean racing embraced another corner of the world, paving the way to new friendships in the sport's vast global family.

Only days earlier, 25,000 fans had descended upon the race village and marina to see in the New Year with a momentous concert by British rockers Coldplay. It was the first of many magical moments in the days that followed.

A headlong sprint down the Emirati coast provided the locals with an electrifying introduction to high-performance sailing.

More than 120,000 came through the gates to take in the atmosphere of the race village. Above all, they came for Azzam and Adil. Azzam – the hometown boat carrying the Arabic name for 'determination' – and Adil Khalid, the hometown boy who personifies that attribute on behalf of a nation.

For the teams, it was an opportunity to unwind with families and reclaim a holiday season missed at sea. Rigging problems suffered on Leg 2 meant that Sanya were not among them. For the Chinese, the opportunity to rejoin the race would come in the maze of fluky conditions and shipping lanes en route to their home port.

SANYA

KNUT FROSTAD, DIGNITARIES

AL FURSAN FLYING TEAM, THE VOLVO OCEAN RACE TROPHY

The official race village opening marks the race's first-ever visit to the Middle East.

L'ouverture officielle du village marque la première visite de la course au Moyen-Orient.

La inauguración oficial del race village marca la primera visita de la regata al golfo Pérsico.

赛事村的开放标志着比赛第一次来到中东地区。

The Emirates' premier aerobatics team 'The Knights' give the race a resounding welcome.

'The Knights' –la première équipe d'acrobatie aérienne des Emirats– accueille la course de façon sensationnelle.

El equipo acrobático emiratí, 'los Caballeros', le dan a la regata una espectacular bienvenida.

享誉阿联酋的飞行特技表演团欢迎赛事到来。

IAN WALKER / ABU DHABI OCEAN RACING

ABU DHABI RACE VILLAGE

A day at the camel races offers the race entourage a chance to sample local culture.

Une journée aux courses de chameau et le milieu de la course goûte à la culture locale.

Un día en las carreras de camellos ofrece al séquito de la regata una oportunidad de saborear las tradiciones locales.

骑骆驼比赛给赛事带来了浓浓的阿拉伯风情。

A sparkling new marina in the heart of the city plays host to the Volvo Open 70s.

Un port flambant neuf au cœur de la ville accueille les Volvo Open 70.

Una reluciente nueva marina a los pies de la ciudad es la anfitriona de los Volvo Open 70.

全新打造的码头内停泊着沃尔沃Open70战舰。

SHEIKH NAHYAN BIN MUBARAK AL NAHYAN, TONY BLAIR

For Abu Dhabi, hosting the race was a high profile statement of its commitment to top level sport.

Pour Abu Dhabi, recevoir la course est l'occasion d'affirmer son intérêt dans l'accueil de sports de haut niveau.

Para Abu Dabi, albergar la regata fue una afirmación de su interés en deportes de alto nivel.

阿布扎比通过举办沃尔沃环球帆船赛凸显了对高端体育赛事的浓厚兴趣。

COMMUNICATIONS

Inmarsat technology feeds the race's media platforms while providing the teams with vital connectivity.

La technologie d'Inmarsat fournit plateformes média à la course et liens vitaux aux équipes.

La tecnología de Inmarsat alimenta la plataforma mediática de la regata y provee a los equipos con enlaces fundamentales.

Inmarsat通信卫星公司提供了媒体内容的传输支持，保障了船队与外界的及时联络。

ALASTAIR COOK, GRAEME SWANN

The England cricketers enjoy a break from preparations for their test series opener against Pakistan.

Les joueurs de cricket anglais font une pause dans leur entrainement avant leurs séries avec le Pakistan.

Los jugadores de cricket ingleses disfrutan de un descanso de sus series de partidos contra Paquistán.

英格兰板球队从与巴基斯坦的系列测试赛中抽出身来，造访沃尔沃帆船赛事村。

CHRIS NICHOLSON / CAMPER WITH EMIRATES TEAM NEW ZEALAND

Traditional dhow racing provides a spectacular change of scene for many of the sailors.

La course en boutre traditionnel offre un changement de paysage radical à de nombreux marins.

Una regata de los tradicionales dhow ofrece a los regatistas un espectacular cambio de escenario.

壮观的传统阿拉伯帆船比赛。

Azzam ablaze. Hometown victories provided indelible moments for Abu Dhabi Ocean Racing.

Azzam s'embrase : leurs victoires dans leur port d'attache sont des moments inoubliables pour Abu Dhabi Ocean Racing.

El Azzam fascina. Las victorias en su ciudad natal le dan al Abu Dhabi Ocean Racing momentos inolvidables.

"阿萨姆号"在家门口不负重望，赢得阿布扎比港内赛冠军。

"Today is the single biggest day of the race for us." Ian Walker and crew were on top of the world after a thrilling Etihad Airways In-Port Race victory.

« Aujourd'hui est le plus grand jour de cette course pour nous. » Ian Walker et son équipage après une victoire palpitante sur la course In-Port Etihad Airways.

"Hoy es el día más importante de la regata para nosotros". Ian Walker y su tripulación estaban en las nubes tras una emocionante victoria en la in-port Etihad Airways.

"今天绝对是个大日子"，伊恩·沃克在带领船队赢得港内赛后高兴的说。

Their excellent form continued in the sprint race back to Sharjah. A 16-second winning margin gave Walker's team another perfect points-haul.

Ils continuent de briller lors du sprint retour vers Sharjah, s'imposant à 16 secondes près. Ecart gagnant et opération comptable parfaite pour l'équipe de Walker.

Su excelente forma continuó en la regata hasta Sharjah. Una victoria por 16 segundos de ventaja les dio otra alegría.

阿布扎比队的快乐在重返沙迦的比赛结束后继续，16秒的优势再次为船队赢得胜利，积分也越来越好看。

A repeat of anti-piracy measures saw the fleet again loaded for transit through the danger zone and on to the Stage 2 start line.

Les mesures anti-piraterie sont répétées au retour et la flotte traverse de nouveau la zone dangereuse en cargo pour être au départ de la deuxième partie.

Las medidas antipiratería llevaron a la flota de nuevo al mercante para atravesar la zona de peligro y volver a la línea de salida de la segunda parte.

防海盗措施在船队返程中继续实施，各艘战舰再次登上货轮，回到第二阶段比赛的起点。

A leg restart on Chinese New Year provided a fitting date for Team Sanya to reboot their challenge for points.

L'étape repart le jour du Nouvel An chinois, une date adaptée au retour de Team Sanya, en quête de points.

La etapa se reanuda en el Año Nuevo Chino, fecha perfecta para que el Team Sanya reinicie su búsqueda de puntos.

"三亚号"回归比赛之日正好赶上中国的春节。

A confident start by Telefónica was soon frustrated by a problem with their headsail. Frantic crew work managed to keep their quest for leg victory on track.

Telefónica part confiant mais est vite frustré par un problème de voile d'avant. Le travail acharné de l'équipage leur permet de reprendre leur course pour la victoire.

Una convincente salida del Telefónica se vio frustrada al poco por un problema en su vela de proa. La tripulación trabajó frenéticamente para mantener vivas las opciones de ganar la etapa.

西班牙电信队出发后不久就遇到头帆故障，团队卓绝的努力确保了船队胜利的势头。

Tactical sparring for position and ever-present fishing fleets made the approach to the Strait of Malacca tense and complex.

Positions stratégiques et flotte de pêche omniprésente rendent l'approche du détroit de Malacca tendue et complexe.

Las batallas tácticas y las omnipresentes flotas de pescadores hicieron la ruta hacia el estrecho de Malaca tensa y compleja.

排位大战和恼人的渔网让马六甲海峡的航行紧张而复杂。

Shipping traffic and debris combined with fickle conditions to give the teams much to contend with.

Le trafic maritime, les débris flottants et les conditions changeantes occupent largement les équipages.

El tráfico marítimo, la basura y unas condiciones inestables complicaron mucho las cosas a los equipos.

繁忙的海上交通、漂浮的废物和多变的天气让比赛充满变数。

Out of the strait, tough upwind sailing tested the teams. Groupama pushed hard for the lead all the way but had to settle for second.

Sortis du détroit, un près difficile teste les équipages. Groupama pousse pour prendre la tête mais doit se contenter de la deuxième place.

Saliendo del estrecho, una dura ceñida puso a prueba a los equipos. El Groupama presionó para liderar todo el camino pero se tuvo que conformar con un segundo.

出了马六甲海峡，严酷的迎风航行成为船队的新考验，收官之际的事故让安盟保险队的胜利希望化为泡影。

The sheer number of obstacles made sleep a rare commodity. Experience and cool heads kept crew spirits high.

Tous ces obstacles raréfient le sommeil. C'est l'expérience et le sang-froid qui permettent aux équipiers de garder le moral.

Los obstáculos hicieron que dormir fuera un lujo escaso. La experiencia y mantener la calma mantuvo a las tripulaciones con la moral alta.

航行路上的众多障碍让睡眠成了件奢侈品，丰富的经验和冷静的头脑是重中之重。

Iker Martínez and his crew played the conditions to perfection. Triumphant in Sanya, a hat-trick of leg victories for Telefónica was threatening to turn the race into a procession.

Iker Martínez et son équipage se sont joués des conditions à la perfection. Ils triomphent à Sanya. Le triplé de victoires de Telefónica menace de transformer la course en un cortège.

Iker Martínez y su tripulación manejaron las condiciones a la perfección. Triunfantes en Sanya, con tres victorias consecutivas en las etapas, el Telefónica amenazaba con convertir la regata en una procesión.

伊克尔·马丁内兹和他的队员们将表现发挥到极致，在三亚迎来的胜利让船队上演了"帽子戏法"，也让船队的领先优势难以逆转。

SANYA

4 – 19 Feb 2012
Sanya Haitang Bay In-Port Race: *18 Feb 2012, 07:00 UTC*
Leg 4 Start: *19 Feb 2012, 07:00 UTC*
Official Distance: *5,220 nm*

As the holiday crowds thronged Sanya's Serenity Marina, a tide was rising. A sequence of immaculate performances by Telefónica had forced the rest of the fleet to reassess. Pressure was mounting to halt the Spanish team's charge for the trophy.

Four teams had shared the podium positions on the offshore legs to date, but the blue boat's impressive consistency meant Telefónica were building a significant lead over their rivals. Approaching the halfway point in the race, there were still plenty of points to sail for. But the brains behind PUMA, CAMPER and Groupama knew that Leg 4 was a watershed moment. For them, it was a case of now or never if they were to step up and signal real winning intent.

Iker Martínez and Xabi Fernández had no such concerns. While their opponents fretted, the freshly crowned World Sailors of the Year returned to Spain to clock up valuable training hours in preparation for another tilt at Olympic gold in the 49er class at the London Games.

Hostile conditions in the South China Sea paved the way to 20 days of punishing sailing. Leg 4's breathtaking finish would show just how narrow the margin between first and last place had become in this brave new world of professional ocean racing.

Eye of the Tiger. Teng Jiang He
received a welcome that will long be
remembered.

L'œil du tigre. Un accueil de héros qui
restera dans les mémoires pour Teng
Jiang He.

El Ojo del Tigre. Teng Jiang He recibió
una bienvenida de héroe que será
recordada mucho tiempo.

三亚队队歌叫做《老虎的眼睛》。滕江和
是赛事历史中的首位竞赛船员，在三亚获
得了英雄般的欢迎。

SANYA CITY RECEPTION

SANYA RACE VILLAGE, SERENITY MARINA

A lavish event hosted by TV personality Angela Chow officially welcomes the race to Sanya.

Une cérémonie animée par la star de la télé Angela Chow salue l'arrivée à Sanya.

Una espléndida recepción presentada por la televisiva Angela Chow da la bienvenida oficial de la regata a Sanya.

三亚市政府举行盛大晚宴欢迎船队来到三亚，知名主持人周英琦担任晚宴司仪。

The race got to make first use of Sanya's impressive new marina.

La course est la première à se servir de l'impressionnante nouvelle marina.

La regata estrenó la impresionante marina de Sanya.

赛事启用了三亚全新的帆船码头。

TENG JIANG HE, LOU BAO MING, KNUT FROSTAD

LUO XUEJUAN

Hainan's Party Secretary wishes local hero 'Tiger' well for the racing ahead.

Le secrétaire du parti de Hainan souhaite bon vent à Tiger, le héros local.

El secretario del partido de Hainan le desea al "Tigre", el favorito local, lo mejor en la regata.

海南省委书记罗保铭为中国船员滕江和送行。

China's Olympic champion swimmer guests on board Team Sanya for the Leg 4 start.

La nageuse et championne olympique chinoise invitée à bord de Team Sanya pour le départ de l'étape 4.

La nadadora estrella china es la invitada a bordo del Team Sanya en la salida de la Etapa 4.

"女蛙王"罗雪娟在第四赛段启航时登上"三亚号"。

OPENING CEREMONY, SANYA RACE VILLAGE

Crowds flock to join Sanya's Celebration of Sail.

Le public afflue pour la 'Celebration of Sail' de Sanya.

El público se congrega para la Celebración de la Vela de Sanya.

庆祝"三亚号"抵达的人群。

LIVE ENTERTAINMENT

Colourful performances are a regular event in a memorable stopover.

Des démonstrations colorées, moments fréquents de cette escale mémorable.

Las coloridas actuaciones son un acontecimiento frecuente en una escala memorable.

三亚停靠港上演了丰富的文艺表演。

PRO-AM RACE GUESTS, KEN READ / PUMA

Specially invited guests enjoy a money-can't-buy experience in the Pro-Am racing.

Les invités profitent d'une expérience qui n'a pas de prix lors des courses Pro-Am.

Para los invitados, las pruebas pro-am ofrecen experiencias que el dinero no puede comprar.

混合赛为受邀嘉宾提供了一次难得的体验机会。

YANG WEI

The triple gold-medallist gymnastics star dismounts from CAMPER.

Le gymnaste triple médaillé d'or olympique quitte CAMPER.

El gimnasta tricampeón olímpico se baja del CAMPER.

奥运冠军杨威从看步船上跳下，为船队送行。

Bodhisattva watches. Compassion
was scarce as the teams looked to
lift their game on the 5,220 nm leg to
Auckland.

Sous le regard de Bodhisattva, pas
d'attendrissement : les équipes
doivent hisser leur niveau de jeu
pour cette étape de 5220 milles vers
Auckland.

Bodhisattva observa. La compasión
es escasa cuando los equipos buscan
la victoria en la etapa de 5220 millas
náuticas hasta Auckland.

前往奥克兰的5220海里的赛段让比赛的
激烈程度升级。

Organisers were forced to delay
the leg start as waves described as
'liquid mountain ranges' lay in wait off
Sanya's coast.

Les organisateurs contraints de
retarder le départ de l'étape alors
que des vagues décrites comme 'des
montagnes liquides' les attendent au
large de Sanya.

Las "montañas líquidas" en la costa de
Sanya obligaron a los organizadores
a retrasar la salida hacia el mar de la
China.

南中国海的风暴让第四赛段推迟启航。

There were few comforts for the sailors as relentless, pounding seas dominated the early upwind stages of the leg.

Peu de confort pour les marins alors qu'une mer hachée et implacable domine le début de l'étape.

Hay pocas comodidades para los regatistas en los primeros compases en ceñida de la etapa, dominados por el incansable embate de las olas.

汹涌的海面和迎面而来的大风让比赛一开始就变得异常艰苦。

A dying weather system forced the
fleet to head far into the east in search
of the trade winds that would help
their passage south.

Un système météo mourant force
la flotte à s'éloigner dans l'est pour
chercher les alizés qui l'aideront à
descendre au sud.

Un sistema meteorológico agonizante
obligó a la flota a dirigirse mucho más
al este en búsqueda de los alisios que
les iban a ayudar en su ruta hacia el
sur.

微弱的海风让船队被迫向东航行，寻找帮
助他们南下的贸易风。

Defying everything that the Pacific could throw at them, only two hours separated the last five boats in an epic Auckland finish.

Après avoir affronté tous les obstacles du Pacifique, deux heures seulement séparent les cinq derniers bateaux à Auckland, dans un finish épique.

Desafiando cualquier cosa que el Pacífico les arrojara, solo dos horas separaron a los últimos cinco barcos en una llegada mítica en Auckland.

经过太平洋的一路波折，最后五支抵达奥克兰的赛船前后相差不到两个小时。

Bold tactics and smart repair work meant PUMA's second place was as hard-earned as it was fully deserved. Memories of their Leg 1 woes were slowly fading.

Tactique audacieuse et réparations intelligentes permettent la belle et méritée deuxième place de PUMA. Leurs souvenirs de l'étape 1 s'effacent peu à peu.

Una arriesgada táctica y buena reparación hicieron que el PUMA ganara a pulso su totalmente merecida segunda plaza. El recuerdo de su Etapa 1 se desvanecía poco a poco.

出色的战术运用与高效的维修工作让彪马队在第四赛段中的第二名弥足珍贵，也让第一赛段事故带来的挫败感渐渐消退。

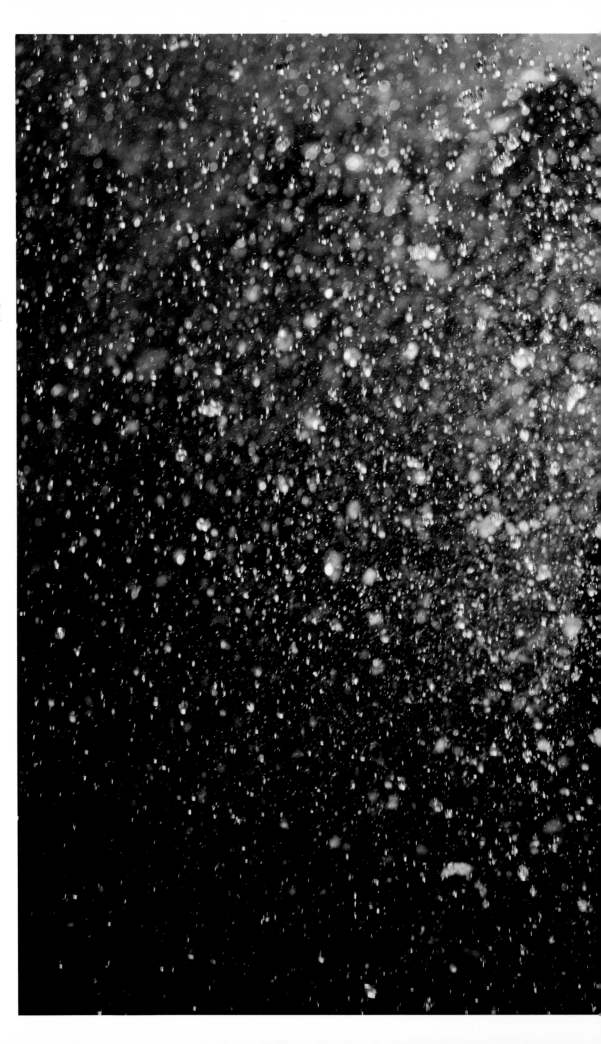

But the applause belonged to Groupama. Victory in Auckland showed the French had found the form hinted at by their pre-race billing as the fastest around the planet.

Mais les applaudissements vont à Groupama. Par leur victoire à Auckland, les Français montrent qu'ils ont trouvé la forme que suggérait leur record de vitesse autour du globe.

Pero el aplauso pertenecía al Groupama 4. La victoria en Auckland demostró que los franceses habían encontrado la fórmula para cumplir con las expectativas de ser los más rápidos alrededor del planeta.

最终的胜利属于"安盟4号"，船队第一个驶入奥克兰，证明了自己不容小觑的实力。

Telefónica's dominance had been dealt a blow as they were forced to battle just to secure third place behind PUMA and Groupama.

La domination de Telefónica prend un coup : ils doivent se battre pour seulement s'assurer la troisième place.

El dominio del Telefónica había recibido un duro golpe al verse obligados a batallar por la tercera plaza.

西班牙电信队落在了彪马队和安盟保险队之后，只能争取保住第三的位置。

SANYA

AUCKLAND

8 – 18 Mar 2012
Auckland In-Port Race: *17 Mar 2012, 01:00 UTC*
Leg 5 Start: *18 Mar 2012, 01:00 UTC*
Official Distance: *6,705 nm*

Since the race's inception in 1973, Southern Ocean legs have commanded a status bordering on mythical. Purists regard them as the true test of a sailor and rounding Cape Horn as a rite of passage for all.

But a lot more than kudos was at stake when the fleet headed back into the vast Pacific. First place and 30 points beckoned, but lay more than half a world away. Between the warmth of Auckland's race village and Itajaí, 6,705 nm away in Brazil, the crews would endure unrelenting discomfort in the Roaring Forties and Furious Fifties.

A racecourse limit was set at 58° South to remove ice and reckless speed from the list of dangers awaiting the fleet.

The events that followed were the best of times and the worst of times. Day after day, reports came in of boats suffering damage at the hands of the ferocious conditions. All but one of the teams would be forced to stop for repairs at some stage and only four would make it to the finish line at all.

When the boats were welcomed by thousands of fans in Itajaí, it was the culmination of a relentlessly dramatic leg. The rest of us could only watch and wonder how a life like this feels.

ITAJAÍ

Even as they enjoyed Auckland's
infectious enthusiasm, the demanding
miles ahead were never far from the
sailors' minds.

L'exigence des milles à venir n'est
jamais loin de l'esprit des marins
- même au moment de profiter
de l'enthousiasme contagieux
d'Auckland.

En medio del contagioso entusiasmo
de Auckland, los regatistas nunca
dejaron de pensar en las exigentes
millas por venir.

一面是奥克兰观众的热情，一面是启航后
恶劣天气的冷峻。

Dazzle ship. CAMPER's hometown supporters had plenty to cheer when they notched their first win in the Auckland In-Port Race.

Bateau éblouissant. Les supporters locaux de CAMPER ont de quoi s'emballer lors de leur première victoire sur la course In-Port d'Auckland.

Los seguidores del CAMPER en su propia ciudad tenían mucho que celebrar cuando llegaron en primera posición en la Auckland In-Port.

迷彩船。看步 · 新西兰酋长队赢得了奥克兰港内赛的冠军，也获得了母港观众最热情的欢呼。

A strong finish in Leg 4 had given Sanya new belief. After a good result in the in-port race, their spirits rose further as they led the fleet out into the Hauraki Gulf.

Un finish satisfaisant sur l'étape 4 a redonné de l'espoir à Sanya. Après un bon résultat sur la course In-Port d'Auckland, ils continuent de briller en menant la flotte à la sortie du golfe d'Hauraki.

Un buen resultado en la Etapa 4 le dio al Team Sanya una nueva ilusión. Tras un buen resultado en la Auckland In-Port Race, la moral se mantuvo alta cuando lideraron la flota en la salida del golfo de Hauraki.

第四赛段的良好表现重新燃起三亚队的斗志，港内赛的良好发挥和率先驶出奥克兰港的表现也为船队平添了不少信心。

Hopes that fortune was now smiling on the Chinese entry died on Day 5 of Leg 5. A rudder tore from its mount and Sanya were once again scrambling for land.

Mais les espoirs du projet chinois s'effondrent le cinquième jour de l'étape 5. Un safran s'arrache de sa fixation et Sanya est de nouveau obligé de rejoindre la terre.

La ilusión de que la fortuna le sonriera al equipo chino murió en la quinta jornada de la Etapa 5. Una pala del timón arrancada y el Sanya de nuevo arrastrándose a tierra.

第五赛段进入第五个比赛日，厄运再次来袭，这艘中国船的船舵发生折断，不得不仓惶靠岸。

The Southern Ocean unleashed classic round-the-world sailing conditions, testing the seamanship of all the teams to the limit.

Le Grand Sud et ses conditions classiques de tour du monde à la voile, pour tester le sens marin de tous les équipages jusqu'à la limite.

El océano Antártico desencadenó las condiciones típicas de una vuelta al mundo, poniendo a prueba la marinería de los equipos hasta el límite.

南大洋制造了最险峻的航行条件，也将每一位船员推到了心理和体能的极限。

"To finish first, first you must finish."
As conditions steadily worsened and
crew-fatigue set in, attention shifted
from speed to survival.

« Pour finir premier, vous devez
d'abord finir. » Les conditions se
dégradent, les équipiers fatiguent et la
priorité passe de la vitesse à la survie.

"Para llegar primero, primero hay que
llegar." Al empeorar las condiciones e
instalarse el agotamiento, el objetivo
cambiaba de velocidad a supervivencia.

"想贏得比賽，必須先比完賽"。随着
海上情况的进一步恶化以及水手们的疲
惫感与日俱增，注意力已经从速度转移
到生存。

A hard fall off a 10-metre wave put CAMPER thousands of miles from land and in need of critical repairs.

Un choc dans une vague de 10 mètres contraint CAMPER à d'indispensables réparations à plusieurs milliers de milles de la terre.

Una dura caída desde una ola de diez metros puso al CAMPER en necesidad de reparaciones críticas lejos de tierra.

十米大浪让看步·新西兰酋长队船只受损，需要紧急维修。

Real fear of breaking apart weighed heavily on CAMPER's crew as they set off on an eight-day trek to safety in Chile.

La crainte de casser le bateau en plusieurs pièces pèse sur CAMPER alors que l'équipe se prépare à huit jours de convoyage vers le Chili.

El miedo real de partir en dos el barco estuvo omnipresente en la tripulación del CAMPER durante una travesía de ocho días hasta llegar a Chile.

为了确保船只安全，船队决定花八天时间停靠智利进行维修。

Soon, Abu Dhabi too were fighting to stay afloat. Frantic efforts to repair damage could not salvage their hopes of getting around Cape Horn intact.

Bientôt, Abu Dhabi se bat lui aussi pour rester à flot. Leurs efforts frénétiques pour réparer ne suffisent pas à leur laisser passer le Cap Horn.

Pronto, el Abu Dhabi también estaba luchando para mantenerse a flote. Los fanáticos esfuerzos de reparar el daño no fueron suficientes para afrontar la furia del Cabo de Hornos.

之后不久，阿布扎比队也遭遇事故，维修船只的迫切性超过了冒险绕过合恩角的希望。

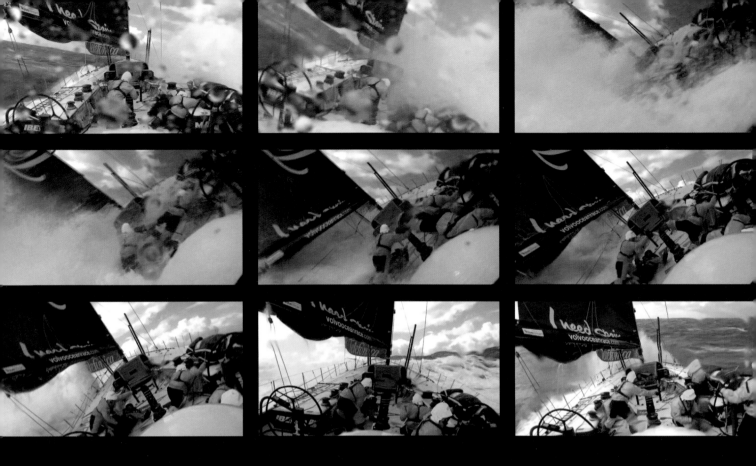

Telefónica were pummelled by vicious seas deep in the Roaring Forties. On board, a decision was made to hold back from mounting any assault on the lead.

Telefónica est malmené par la mer des 40e rugissants. À bord, on décide de freiner et de ne pas attaquer pour la première place.

El Telefónica fue golpeado por la furia del mar en los Cuarenta Rugientes. A bordo, se tomó la decisión de contener cualquier intento de liderar la etapa.

西班牙电信队在南纬四十度遭遇大浪堵截，船员们不得不变得小心翼翼，不敢再和大浪硬碰硬。

With under 700 nm remaining, Groupama became yet another casualty. Whilst leading the fragmented fleet to Itajaí, another mast came crashing down.

À moins de 700 milles de l'arrivée, Groupama est une nouvelle victime. Ils mènent la flotte restante vers Itajaí quand leur mât tombe.

Con menos de 700 millas náuticas para llegar, el Groupama fue la siguiente baja. Mientras lideraban la mellada flota hacia Itajaí, otro mástil se vino abajo.

在距离终点700海里处，领航的安盟保险队成为又一支遭遇不测的劲旅，船上桅杆发生断裂。

The French arrived in Itajaí late but defiant. Determined not to let their broken mast dent their leaderboard ambitions, they looked towards the future.

Les Français arrivent à Itajaí plus tard que prévu, mais avec panache. Ils n'ont pas l'intention de laisser leur mât cassé briser leurs ambitions et se tournent vers le futur.

Los franceses llegaron a Itajaí tarde pero desafiantes. Determinados a no permitir que un mástil roto estropeara sus ambiciones en la clasificación, miraban al futuro.

法国船队最终排除万难，成功抵达伊塔加，岸队通过努力工作最小化桅杆事故对船队今后表现的影响。

After 20 days of blistering ocean
racing, Leg 5 was transformed into a
match race. Amazingly Telefónica had
come through a late stop for repairs to
draw within 1 nm of PUMA.

Après 20 jours d'une course au large
féroce, l'étape 5 tourne au match-
race. Telefónica réussit à revenir à un
mille de PUMA après avoir dû s'arrêter
pour réparer.

Tras veinte días de devastadora
navegación oceánica, la Etapa 5
se había reducido a un match race.
Increíblemente, el Telefónica había
superado una parada técnica en
Hornos para situarse a una milla
náutica del PUMA.

在20天的怒海争锋后，第五赛段在末尾
呈现了一场西班牙电信队和彪马队之间
的激烈较量。

Monster among men. A battered and bruised Mar Mostro arrived into Itajaí as the only team not to make a pitstop. Textbook seamanship distinguished PUMA's tense victory over Telefónica.

Un monstre parmi les hommes. Seul bateau à ne pas s'être arrêté, un Mar Mostro abimé et fatigué arrive à Itajaí. Un sens marin exemplaire permet à PUMA de prendre la victoire à l'arrachée devant Telefónica.

Monstruos entre los hombres. Un Mar Mostro maltrecho y magullado llegó a Itajaí como el único equipo que no tuvo que parar. Un distinguido saber hacer marinero le dio al PUMA una victoria de infarto sobre el Telefónica.

出色的航海技术和不折不挠的精神让彪马队随然伤痕累累，却成为唯一一支在本赛段中没有靠岸维修的船队，这让他们的胜利格外珍贵并值得尊敬。

ITAJAÍ

4 – 22 Apr 2012
DHL In-Port Race: *21 Apr 2012, 17:00 UTC*
Leg 6 Start: *22 Apr 2012, 17:00 UTC*
Official Distance: *4,800 nm*

After Leg 5's heart-stopping drama, the easy-going air of Itajaí was pure therapy. While the stricken Sanya sped from New Zealand by ship in a bid to reunite with the race in Miami, the other teams used the Brazilian layover to patch up wounds and take stock of the race.

Telefónica's offshore stranglehold had finally been broken a month previously by Groupama and now PUMA too had shown the blue boat could be beaten. No one was about to write off Telefónica as a spent force, however. Their thrilling comeback over the last 1,500 nm into Itajaí had seen them denied a near impossible victory by a whisker. It was a herculean effort that again served to remind of the on-going threat they posed.

In theory, a 20-point cushion at the top of the leaderboard gave Martínez and his crew the luxury of choosing to sail hard for the finish, or to keep their opponents in check. In reality, their opponents were getting far too good and too confident in their boats to have terms dictated to them. The three leading chasers were now swarming and the race leaders were beginning to make mistakes.

In the space of 17 days, Leg 6 would go on to turn the established order of the leaderboard on its head and cast the race in a completely different light. Already the longest and, perhaps, toughest edition in the history of the Volvo Ocean Race, the 2011-12 race was rapidly taking shape as the closest ever.

MIAMI

DHL IN-PORT RACE PRIZE GIVING CEREMONY

Crowds gather
to share in
Groupama's in-
port race triumph.

Le public se
rassemble pour le
triomphe In-Port
de Groupama.

Una multitud
se reúne para
compartir el
triunfo del
Groupama en la
in-port.

观众们庆祝安盟
保险队的港内赛
胜利。

ITAJAÍ, SANTA CATARINA

Itajaí's idyllic bay
provided the race
with a much-
needed break.

La baie
paradisiaque
d'Itajaí, une pause
nécessaire pour la
course.

La idílica bahía
de Itajaí le dio
a la regata un
bien merecido
descanso.

伊塔加宁静美丽的
港湾为赛事和船队
提供了良好休整
条件。

CREW / GROUPAMA SAILING TEAM

The Cape
Town–Cape Horn
winners receive
the Roaring
Forties Trophy.

Les vainqueurs
du Cap – Cap
Horn reçoivent le
Trophée des 40e
Rugissants.

Los ganadores
de Ciudad del
Cabo–Cabo de
Hornos reciben el
Trofeo Cuarenta
Rugientes.

安盟保险队接过第
五赛段奖杯。

WISDOM THE ALBATROSS, PEQUENO ANJO HOSPITAL

The race's Keep
the Oceans Clean!
mascot brings
cheer to local
children.

La mascotte
de Keep the
Oceans Clean
enthousiasme
les enfants de la
région.

La mascota de los
océanos limpios
de la regata lleva
alegría a los niños.

赛事环保吉祥物 "
聪聪" 为当地儿童
带来欢乐。

MIKE PAMMENTER / CAMPER WITH EMIRATES TEAM NZ

The South African bowman and boat captain is snapped by local fans.

Le numéro un et boat captain sud-africain attire les fans locaux.

Aficionados locales se sacan fotos con el proa y capitán del barco sudafricano.

这位来自南非的前甲板手和技术船员在当地拥有众多热情的粉丝。

ROBYN HILTON

Personal medical treatment awaits injured sailor Brad Marsh from his girlfriend.

Un traitement médical personnalisé attend l'équipier Brad Marsh au ponton.

La novia del regatista lesionado Brad Marsh le espera para darle tratamiento médico en el pantalán.

布莱德·马什在停靠港接受治疗。

KEEP THE OCEANS CLEAN!

Itajaí embraces the race's cause with a wide range of initiatives, including a local beach clean.

Itajaí participe via de nombreuses initiatives, dont le nettoyage d'une plage de la région.

Itajaí abraza la causa de la regata con un amplio abanico de iniciativas, incluyendo la limpieza de una playa.

伊塔加在赛事停靠期间举行了多场活动，包括对当地海滩的义务清洁。

TRY SAILING, VOLVO OCEAN RACE EXPERIENCE

Itajaí volunteers are among more than 10,000 to take up the opportunity to learn sailing.

Les bénévoles d'Itajaí sont parmi les plus de 10 000 personnes à apprendre la voile.

Los voluntarios de Itajaí están entre los más de 10 000 que utilizan la regata para aprender sobre vela.

包括伊塔加的志愿者们在内的一万多人通过帆船赛的到来了解了帆船运动。

The punishing leg to Itajaí and the demanding racing ahead meant round-the-clock work on the battered fleet.

Une étape éprouvante vers Itajaí et une course exigeante à venir, et les bateaux sont réparés jour et nuit.

La dura etapa hasta Itajaí y la exigente competición que tenían por delante implicaba trabajar a contrarreloj en la maltrecha flota.

魔鬼赛段和接下来马不停蹄的比赛让岸队有不少工作要做。

The late arrival of three boats forced major logistics and repair efforts into a wickedly narrow timeframe.

L'arrivée tardive de trois bateaux entraine une logistique et des réparations lourdes en un temps limité.

La tardía llegada de tres barcos obligó a realizar trabajos de logística y esfuerzos de reparación en un corto período de tiempo.

由于三支船队晚到，岸队成员只有很少的时间对船只进行维修。

An unforced error by Team Telefónica in the DHL In-Port Race allowed the pursuing teams to pounce on crucial points in Itajaí.

Une erreur involontaire de Team Telefónica sur la course In-Port DHL à Itajaí, et leurs poursuivants se jettent sur ces points cruciaux.

Un error no forzado del Telefónica en la regata DHL In-Port permitió a los perseguidores sumar importantes puntos en Itajaí.

低级失误导致西班牙电信队在伊塔加港内赛中名落孙山。

The teams exorcised the ghosts of Leg 5 in glorious sailing conditions up the South American coast.

Dans les belles conditions de navigation de la côte sud-américaine, les équipages laissent derrière eux les fantômes de l'étape 5.

Los equipos exorcizaron los fantasmas de la Etapa 5 con las excelentes condiciones al subir la costa de Suramérica.

第六赛段的风和日丽与第五赛段的狂风巨浪形成鲜明对比。

Consistently swift winds saw the Volvo Open 70s sailing in their sweet-spot over long periods.

Vents rapides et constants sur de longues périodes de temps, des conditions idéales pour les Volvo Open 70.

Vientos rápidos y consistentes vieron a los Volvo Open 70 navegar en su salsa durante largos períodos.

持续强劲的海风让沃尔沃Open70大帆船性能发挥到最佳。

It was vintage sailing, mercifully without crisis. Maintaining a narrow lead most of the way, PUMA were energised by their recent successes.

De la voile à l'ancienne, clémente et sans crise. Galvanisé par ses récents succès, PUMA maintient tout du long une petite avance.

Fue una navegación excelente y sin incidentes. Un revitalizado PUMA animado por los éxitos recientes lideró por un estrecho margen la mayoría del camino.

这是一段没有事故的完美航行，彪马队继续良好的势头，一路领航。

Only 70 nm separated the fleet as they prepared for a tactical chess game in the calm of the Caribbean.

Seulement 70 milles séparent la flotte qui se prépare à un jeu d'échecs tactique dans le calme des Caraïbes.

Sólo 70 millas náuticas separaron a la flota mientras se preparaban para un intenso juego táctico en la calma del Caribe.

加勒比海的弱风区域打乱了各支船队的步伐，令首尾两支船队的距离缩小到70海里。

Groupama again showed flair. A decision to swing round the Turks and Caicos Islands became the passing manoeuvre that sealed third place.

Groupama montre de nouveau son talent. En décidant de contourner les îles Turks et Caicos, ils se garantissent la troisième place.

El Groupama volvió a mostrar su arte. Una decisión de rodear las islas Turcos y Caicos se convirtió en la maniobra clave de adelantamiento que selló la tercera plaza.

安盟保险队再次发威，一次有效的战略调整让船队成功挤入三甲。

PUMA held off a persistent drive from CAMPER to claim back-to-back leg honours in Miami. A string of second places wasn't exactly what CAMPER wanted but the results underlined their consistency.

PUMA doit faire face à un CAMPER obstiné qui voudrait bien prendre la victoire à Miami. Car même si elles prouvent la constance de l'équipage, ses deuxièmes places l'inquiètent.

El PUMA mantuvo a raya una larga y persistente persecución del CAMPER para obtener en Miami la segunda victoria consecutiva. Una serie de segundos puestos inquietaba al CAMPER pero hablaba muy bien de su consistencia.

彪马队成功抵制了看步的长距离追赶，在迈阿密迎来赛段胜利，而一系列第二名的成绩让看步队心有不甘，但也从另一个侧面显示了船队表现的稳定。

As the race's top four teams finished in perfect, reverse sequence, the leaderboard was transformed. With more than 33,000 nm gone, a mere 17 points now separated the leading quartet.

Les quatre premiers terminent exactement dans l'ordre inverse du général et le classement se transforme. Plus de 33 000 milles sont passés et seuls 17 points séparent désormais le quatuor de tête.

Los cuatro primeros llegaron en una formación invertida perfecta, transformando la clasificación. Con más de 33 000 millas náuticas de regata completadas, solo 17 puntos separaban a los cuatro primeros equipos.

积分榜上排在前四位的船队逆序抵达迈阿密，积分榜悄然发生着变化。比赛还剩33000海里，第一名和第四名船队只相差17分。

ITAJAÍ

MIAMI

6 – 20 May 2012
PORTMIAMI In-Port Race: *19 May 2012, 17:00 UTC*
Leg 7 Start: *20 May 2012, 17:00 UTC*
Official Distance: *3,590 nm*

In November 2011, the fleet had set off from Spain on level terms – the finish line a world away. Six months later, the race was heading back to the Iberian peninsula with almost nothing separating the top four and a gripping finish in prospect. For the main contenders, the departure from Miami was virtually a race restart.

If the race was wide open, the margin of error was shrinking rapidly. Points won were also points denied to rivals and, from now on, several duels within the fleet had the potential to significantly alter the leaderboard.

It was clear that no one could afford a repeat of the issues that had proved so costly in the first half of the race. From now on, even a temporary setback had the power to inflict irreparable damage on an entire campaign. More than ever, the crews' vigilance would be called upon, especially as the skippers were coming under increasing pressure to seize any opportunity to snare valuable points.

With the clouds gathering on Telefónica's lead, forces of Nature loomed off the Florida coast. Tropical Storm Alberto showed complete disregard for the complexities already confronting the teams. For those of us following the race from the comfort of dry land, it provided yet another thrilling edge to the prospect of the fleet's return to Europe.

LISBON

Sanya were back, keen to prove points as well as earn some. Their costly rudder loss in Leg 5 had placed their efforts on hold for nearly two months.

Sanya est de retour. Ils ont envie de marquer des points et de faire leurs preuves : leur avarie de safran sur l'étape 5 a suspendu leur course pendant presque deux mois.

El Sanya había vuelto, dispuesto a demostrar su valía y a sumar puntos. La pérdida de la pala del timón en la Etapa 5 había paralizado sus esfuerzos durante casi dos meses.

"三亚号"重新回归比赛，期待能够改变船队之前的不佳表现，第五赛段船舵的事故让他们离开比赛将近两个月时间。

Ian Walker and Azzam hit a high as they recorded a third in-port race win in Miami.

En coupant la ligne d'arrivée à Miami, Ian Walker et Azzam signent un triplé de victoires sur les courses In-Port.

Ian Walker y el Azzam sobresalientes al anotar una tercera victoria en la in-port de Miami.

迈阿密港內赛是阿布扎比队赢得的第三场港内赛胜利。

Nothing was going Telefónica's way. Tactical errors and a penalty turn meant they left for Europe only one point better off.

Rien ne va plus pour Telefónica. Des erreurs tactiques et un tour de pénalité leur font quitter l'Europe avec un point d'avance seulement.

Mientras, nada estaba yendo bien para el Telefónica. Errores tácticos y una vuelta de penalización hicieron que partieran hacia Europa con solo un punto de ventaja.

与此同时，西班牙电信队似乎诸事不顺，战术失误和犯规让船队在迈阿密港内赛中仅获得一分。

Miami delivered the teams straight
into the path of Tropical Storm Alberto.
The first storm of the hurricane
season proved a major headache.

Dès la sortie de Miami, la tempête
tropicale Alberto coupe la route des
concurrents. La première tempête de
la saison est un vrai casse-tête.

Desde Miami los equipos entraron
directamente en la tormenta tropical
Alberto. La primera tormenta de la
temporada de huracanes demostró
ser un gran obstáculo.

一离开迈阿密，船队就撞上了阿尔伯托
热带风暴，这成为船队行进道路上的巨
大障碍。

Alberto was a moving target that added to the navigators' woes. The crews were constantly on alert as winds and currents buffeted the teams' fortunes.

Alberto est une cible mobile qui ajoute aux soucis des navigateurs. Sans compter que les équipages, en alerte, sont aussi soumis aux vents et aux courants.

Alberto se movía continuamente dándoles a los navegantes un quebradero de cabeza. Las tripulaciones estaban en alerta constante y los vientos y las corrientes zarandearon la suerte de los equipos.

由于阿尔伯托飓风一直在移动，不仅导航员犯了难，其他水手们也需要时刻警惕风浪的变化。

For the first time, all the boats completed more than 500 nm in a day. With no obvious speed advantage, Abu Dhabi still managed to squeeze out a handy lead with shrewd sailing.

Pour la première fois, tous les bateaux parcourent plus de 500 milles en une journée. Sans être très rapide, mais à la force d'une navigation habile, Abu Dhabi prend une jolie avance.

Por primera vez en la regata, todos los barcos rompieron la barrera de las 500 millas náuticas. Sin tener un barco en principio más veloz, el Abu Dhabi se coló en cabeza a base de navegar con astucia.

在本赛段中，第一次所有船队都突破了24小时行驶500海里的大关，阿布扎比队通过精细的谋兵布局在横穿大西洋的比赛中领航。

At the wheel of CAMPER, the five-race veteran 'Chuny' Bermúdez swerved at high speed to avoid a passing whale.

'Chuny' Bermúdez, cinq éditions au compteur, fait un écart à haute vitesse à la barre de CAMPER pour éviter une baleine.

Al timón del CAMPER, el veterano de cinco ediciones, 'Chuny' Bermudez, cambia de rumbo a gran velocidad para evitar chocar contra una ballena.

第五次参赛的看步船员罗伯托·楚尼在掌舵时紧急避开鲸鱼，成功避免了一起事故的发生。

Telefónica were not so lucky. In
the North Atlantic sleigh-ride, a
collision damaged one of the boat's
daggerboards, leaving them unable to
challenge for victory.

Telefónica n'est pas aussi chanceux.
En Atlantique nord, une collision abîme
l'une des dérives du bateau, rendant la
victoire inaccessible.

El Telefónica no tuvo tanta suerte.
En la velocidad del Atlántico Norte,
una colisión dañó una de las orzas
de deriva del barco, incapacitándolos
para obtener la victoria.

西班牙人再次遭遇不幸，他们在北大西洋
的航行中损坏了船只的中插板，让胜利的
希望灰飞烟灭。

Abu Dhabi held off Groupama throughout the final days of a memorable leg. A nerve-wracking victory in the Lisbon night capped a great performance by Azzam.

Abu Dhabi tient Groupama à distance lors des derniers jours d'une étape mémorable. Belle performance pour Azzam, vainqueur sur le fil dans la nuit de Lisbonne.

Ian Walker aguantó una persecución despiadada del Groupama que duró días. La victoria por los pelos del Azzam en la noche lisboeta coronó una magnífica actuación.

伊恩·沃克成功钳制了来自安盟队的追赶，"阿萨姆号"终于在夜晚时分抵达里斯本，赢得第七赛段的胜利。

Iker Martínez and his men had to fight all the way up the Tagus River to salvage fourth place. It wasn't enough to prevent a tidal shift in the race standings.

Iker Martínez et ses hommes se battent tout au long du fleuve Tage pour sauver la quatrième place - pas assez pourtant pour arrêter les changements du classement.

Iker Martínez y sus hombres tuvieron que luchar en su subida por el Tajo para salvar su cuarto puesto. No fue suficiente para evitar el cambio en la clasificación general.

伊克尔·马丁内兹和队友们在塔古斯河口艰难的航行，希望确保赛段第四名的位置，然而这已经无法改变船队掉下积分榜首的命运了。

Tenacity had become a hallmark of Groupama's race. Arriving second into Lisbon meant that, for the first time since Cape Town, the race had a new overall leader.

La ténacité est devenue une caractéristique de Groupama. À Lisbonne, leur deuxième place offre un nouveau leader à la course pour la première fois depuis Le Cap.

La tenacidad se convirtió en el estandarte de la regata del Groupama. El segundo puesto al llegar a Lisboa significó que por primera vez desde Ciudad del Cabo, la regata tenía un nuevo líder de la general.

坚持不懈是安盟保险队表现的最佳注解，第七赛段第二名的成绩让船队荣登积分榜首，自开普敦以来，积分榜首的船队第一次发生了变化。

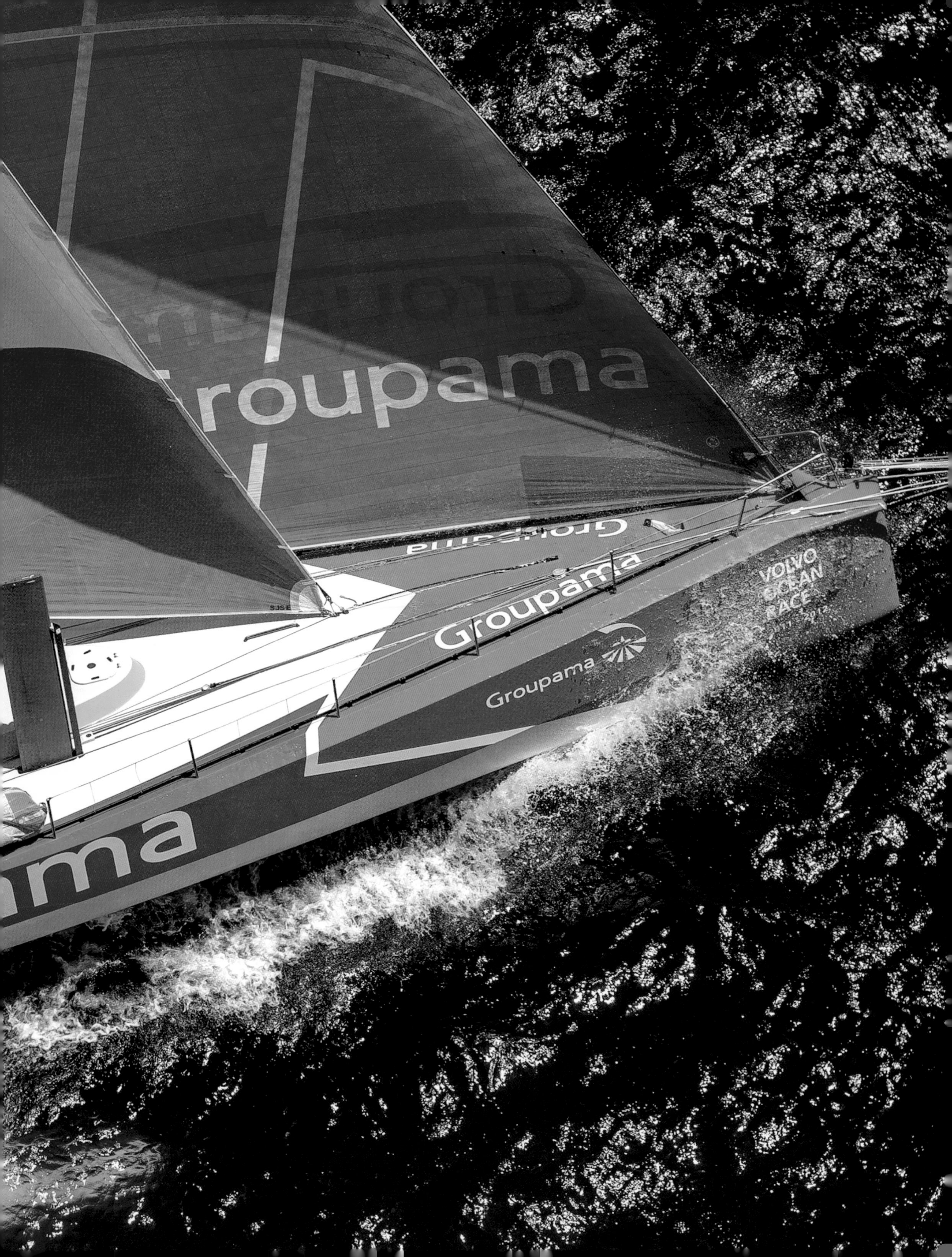
Groupama
Groupama
Groupama
VOLVO OCEAN RACE

LISBON

31 May – 10 June 2012
Oeiras In-Port Race: *9 June 2012, 12:00 UTC*
Leg 8 Start: *10 June 2012, 12:00 UTC*
Official Distance: *1,940 nm*

It was fitting that Lisbon – a city so steeped in maritime heritage – should play host to a race that was ready to make history. Over its four decades, the world's premier ocean race had often been the scene of great drama, but it had never known a contest quite like this.

Leg 8 was compelling for many reasons, but the prospect of the duel between Groupama and Telefónica gave it a special edge. Only three points separated two teams that were headed into a part of the world each regarded as its home turf. Each knew that a single error might wipe out years of preparation in an instant. The added risk of being brushed aside by PUMA or CAMPER, or swept out of contention altogether by the unforgiving Bay of Biscay, only added to the intrigue.

On paper, Leg 8 appeared simple enough: the 1,940 nm course demanded only two major manoeuvres from the teams. But at sea level, the conditions were considerably less straightforward. World-class tactics and seamanship were called for.

It promised to be a true test of the modern-day professional sailor. With everything to play for, and only the raw, unbridled power of a Volvo Open 70 to do it on, this was no place for the faint-hearted.

As the fleet buckled itself in for its high-stakes rollercoaster ride, tension filled Lisbon's race village. In a little under five days, another drama would play out in the great saga of the race – one that would maybe live on in memories for 40 years more.

PRESIDENT CAVACO SILVA, JOÃO LAGOS, DIGNITARIES

The presidential couple joins the mayors of Oeiras and Lisbon to mark the race's first visit to Portugal.

Le couple présidentiel rejoint les maires d'Oeiras et de Lisbonne pour saluer la première visite de la course au Portugal.

La pareja presidencial se une a los alcaldes de Oeiras y Lisboa para señalar la primera visita de la regata a Portugal.

总统夫妇和里斯本市长共同出席活动，欢迎沃尔沃环球帆船赛首次造访葡萄牙。

PRINCE FELIPE OF SPAIN

The former sailing Olympian visits and lends his support to Team Telefónica.

L'ancien régatier olympique affiche son soutien à Team Telefónica.

El que fuera regatista olímpico visita y da su apoyo al Telefónica.

前奥运帆船冠军来到赛事村，为西班牙电信队加油。

TRADITIONAL CANOAS

Few major cities enjoy deeper connections with sailing than the Portuguese capital.

Peu de grandes villes sont aussi liées à la voile que la capitale portugaise.

Pocas grandes ciudades tienen una relación tan profunda con la vela.

里斯本与航海和帆船运动的渊源颇深。

THERESA ZABELL

The double Olympic champion joins her compatriots on board.

La double championne olympique rejoint ses compatriotes à bord.

La doble campeona olímpica se une a sus compatriotas a bordo.

奥运会帆船比赛两枚金牌得主为本国船队加油。

CRISTO REI OVERLOOKING THE TAGUS RIVER

Lisbon's natural amphitheatre provides a spectacular sailing stage.

L'amphithéâtre naturel de Lisbonne, spectaculaire décor pour la régate.

El anfiteatro natural de Lisboa ofrece un escenario espectacular.

里斯本的河港为比赛提供了美丽的背景。

LUIS FIGO, CREW / ABU DHABI OCEAN RACING

An adoring crowd looks on as the football icon joins Azzam for the leg start.

Un public de fans regarde alors que l'icône du football monte à bord d'Azzam pour le départ.

Los aficionados observan al ídolo del fútbol que se une al Azzam para la salida de la etapa.

赛段启航前，足球巨星菲戈登上阿布扎比队的"阿萨姆号"。

KARIN BÄCKLUND, MAYOR ANTONIO COSTA

Interactive exhibits provide a popular attraction in the race village.

Des expositions interactives, attractions populaires sur le village.

Las exposiciones interactivas son una atracción popular en el race village.

赛事村内的互动展示吸引了不少游客。

NRP SAGRES III

The Oeiras In-Port Race takes place in the shadow of the tall ship.

La course In-Port Oeiras se déroule à l'ombre du navire.

La regata Oeiras In-Port tiene lugar a la sombra de la fragata.

里斯本港内赛在一艘巨大的帆船前打响。

Groupama showed no sign of nerves, taking maximum points from the Oeiras In-Port Race and extending their overall lead.

Groupama, impassible, prend le maximum de points sur la course In-Port Oeiras. L'équipe creuse son avance au général.

El Groupama demostró tener nervios de acero al llevarse el máximo número de puntos de la regata Oeiras In-Port, extendiendo así su liderato.

安盟保险队拿下港内赛，进一步巩固了积分榜首的地位。

It was another day to forget for Telefónica. A controversial penalty left them languishing at the rear of the fleet.

Une autre journée à oublier pour Telefónica. Une pénalité controversée les laisse en queue de flotte.

Otro día para olvidar para el Telefónica. Una controvertida penalización les dejó languideciendo en la cola de la flota.

西班牙电信队再次迎来失败日，由于犯规，船队又一次排在了港内赛的最后一位。

The teams rode the Azores High out to the turning mark at the island of São Miguel. The sense of anticipation was immense.

Les équipages passent l'anticyclone des Açores en enroulant l'île de São Miguel. L'impatience est palpable.

Los equipos se subieron al anticiclón la de las Azores en la isla de San Miguel. Todos tenían grandes expectativas.

船队穿过亚速尔高压，绕过圣·米盖尔岛，全速向终点前进。

With only 10 nm separating the fleet, a 'perfect' low pressure system was forming over the Bay of Biscay with almost poetic timing.

10 milles seulement séparent les concurrents et une dépression 'parfaite' se forme sur le golfe de Gascogne – un timing quasi poétique.

Con solo 10 millas náuticas separando a los equipos, un sistema "perfecto" de bajas presiones se estaba formando en el golfo de Vizcaya.

首尾船队距离只有10海里，而比斯开湾内形成的低压带正好给船队送来了期待已久的风力。

A wild ride beckoned for the final 1,200 nm blast to Lorient. How hard dare the teams push boats and bodies in the hunt for crucial points?

Une chevauchée sauvage s'annonce pour les 1200 milles avant Lorient. Jusqu'où les marins pousseront-ils bateaux et humains dans la chasse aux points ?

Las últimas 1200 millas hasta Lorient fueron salvajes. ¿Cuánto más se atreverían a apretar a los machacados barcos y cuerpos en la lucha por unos puntos cruciales?

冲向洛里昂的最后1200海里，各支船队不惜一切代价赢得宝贵的分数。

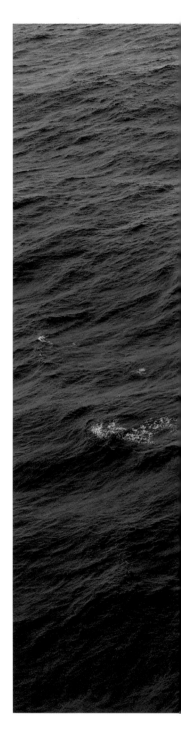

Winds consistently over 40 knots saw blistering speeds. On board PUMA's Mar Mostro, Ken Read was desperate to win and finally wipe out the legacy of Leg 1.

Le vent dépasse les 40 nœuds et les vitesses sont folles. À bord du Mar Mostro de PUMA, Ken Read veut désespérément gagner et se débarrasser des souvenirs de l'étape 1.

Unos vientos constantes de más de 40 nudos provocaron velocidades vertiginosas. A bordo del Mar Mostro, Ken Read estaba desesperado por atacar a la flota y finalmente desquitarse del legado de la Etapa 1.

强劲的海风制造了超过四十节的速度，在彪马队的赛船上，肯·里德带领船队拼命航行，期望最大程度降低第一赛段退赛对船队总成绩的影响。

CAMPER first lost, then regained pole position in the IWC Schaffhausen Speed Record Challenge. They had sailed a staggering 565.84 nm in 24 hours.

CAMPER perd le premier avant de reprendre la main grâce au Record de Vitesse IWC Schaffhausen. L'équipage parcourt 565,84 milles en 24 heures.

El CAMPER primero perdió, luego volvió a colocarse en cabeza en el IWC Schaffhausen Speed Record Challenge. Había navegado 565,84 millas náuticas en 24 horas.

看步·新西兰酋长队以24小时行驶566.84海里的惊人成绩赢得了"IWC沙夫豪森速度挑战赛"。

Groupama were in danger when their mainsail jammed in the extreme conditions. Heroic efforts by bowman Brad Marsh miraculously got the French team through unscathed.

Groupama est menacé lorsque sa grand-voile se coince dans des conditions extrêmes, mais les efforts héroïques de Brad Marsh permettent à l'équipe française de s'en sortir indemne.

El Groupama 4 en peligro cuando su vela mayor se enredó en condiciones extremas. Gracias a los heroicos esfuerzos del proa, Brad Marsh, el equipo francés salió ileso.

安盟保险队的主帆在极端天气下被卡住，前甲板手布莱德·马什通过英勇的高空作业为船队化险为夷。

A colossal leg performance by Team Telefónica lay in ruins when three broken rudders struck in the space of six hours. Only a miracle could get them back into contention now.

La superbe performance de Team Telefónica est réduite à néant par trois safrans cassés en l'espace de six heures. Seul un miracle peut désormais les ramener dans la course.

Una colosal actuación del Telefónica en la etapa se hace añicos al sufrir la rotura de tres timones en seis horas. Solo un milagro podría llevarlos de nuevo a la contienda.

西班牙电信队六小时内三只船舵发生损坏，彻底毁掉了船队之前的出色表现，想要获胜，除非有奇迹发生。

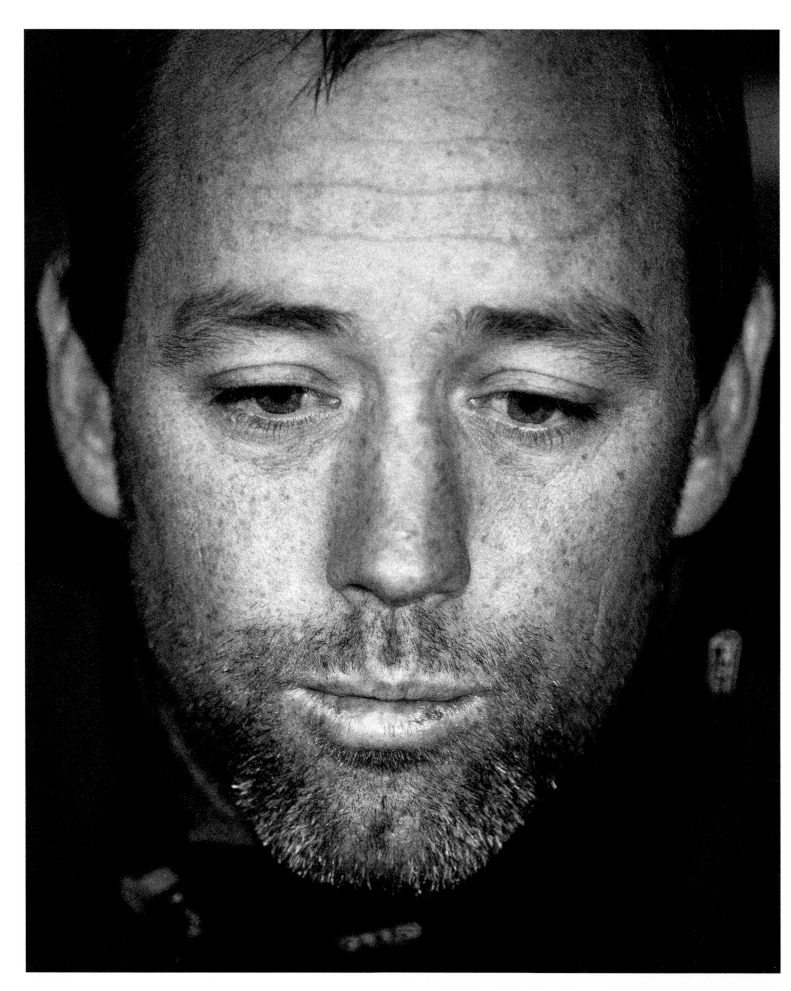

"We dreamed of arriving first into Lorient." For Franck Cammas, a dream lay fulfilled. Much more, the Volvo Ocean Race trophy was now within reach.

« Nous rêvions d'arriver premiers à Lorient. » Pour Franck Cammas, un rêve se réalise. Plus que ça : le trophée de la Volvo Ocean Race est maintenant à sa portée.

"Soñábamos con llegar primeros a Lorient." Para Franck Cammas, un sueño cumplido, y mucho más, el trofeo Volvo Ocean Race al alcance de la mano.

"我们一直都梦想能第一个抵达洛里昂"，弗兰科·卡马斯说。现在，沃尔沃环球帆船赛总冠军的奖杯对于安盟保险队来说已经唾手可得了。

"It's like two years' work just disappearing in a matter of minutes. What a mess." Telefónica's ill fortune was crushing for Iker Martínez and his men.

« Deux ans de travail disparaissent en quelques minutes. Quel désastre. » La malchance de Telefónica est fatale à Iker Martínez et ses hommes.

"Es como si el trabajo de dos años desapareciera en cuestión de minutos ¡Qué desastre!" La mala fortuna del Telefónica fue demoledora para Iker Martínez y sus hombres.

"两年的付出和努力就在一瞬间付之东流了，情况和形势真是乱如麻"，伊克尔·马丁内兹感慨船队的糟糕运气，这一赛段中的事故对于西班牙电信队来说是一次致命的打击。

LISBON

LORIENT

16 June – 1 July 2012
Bretagne In-Port Race: *30 June 2012, 11:02 UTC*
Leg 9 Start: *1 July 2012, 11:02 UTC*
Official Distance: *485 nm*

For the fleet of weary men, eight months of travelling the world in Extreme Class was about to come to an end.

From the first night, severe conditions had regularly placed boats and bodies under enormous strains. The fleet's rampaging approach to Lorient was yet another reminder of the challenges modern sailors face just to contain the raw power of today's high-performance boats.

Weather and punishing seas had certainly left a mark on this race, but the 11th edition of the Volvo Ocean Race was truly defined by the unrelenting competitiveness of the sailors themselves. Sheer desire to win had made this – the longest race of all – the most physically and mentally demanding as well.

A large and vocal crowd packed the race village in Lorient. They came as devotees of sailing to salute the spirit and sacrifice of the crews, and to cheer on their local heroes.

Franck Cammas and his team had set out to match themselves against the very best and, with only one leg remaining, they were poised to win the Volvo Ocean Race. Arrival into Galway in the top four would be enough to seal victory.

Behind Groupama, an almighty battle lay in store for PUMA, CAMPER and Telefónica, separated by a mere six points. For them, the dream of overall victory was still flickering but the nightmare of being beaten to a place on the podium loomed larger. Never had the margin between glory and failure been so narrow.

As one crowd dispersed in Lorient, another amassed in Galway. A sailing epic was reaching its conclusion and the people of Galway were determined to celebrate it in legendary Irish fashion. Shortly before 2am local time on July 3, their opportunity arrived.

GALWAY

30 June – 8 July 2012
Discover Ireland In-Port Race: *7 July 2012, 12:00 UTC*

01:49:11

PATROUILLE DE FRANCE, LORIENT RACE VILLAGE

The French Air Force's precision flying team wows the crowds gathered in Brittany.

Plein les yeux. La Patrouille de France devant la foule rassemblée en Bretagne.

La precisión del equipo de vuelo de la Fuerza Aérea Francesa cautiva al público en Bretaña.

法国空军特技队为观众奉上精彩的空中表演。

NEW YACHT CLASS ANNOUNCEMENT, CITÉ DE LA VOILE ÉRIC TABARLY

Among the delegates attending the official briefing, former winning skipper, Grant Dalton.

Parmi les représentants présents au briefing officiel, l'ancien skipper et vainqueur Grant Dalton.

El excampeón, Grant Dalton, se une a la directiva del equipo para la reunión informativa oficial.

前沃尔沃知名水手格兰特·道尔顿参加了赛事官方说明会。

CHRIS NICHOLSON, MIKE SANDERSON, FRANCK CAMMAS

The Groupama skipper plays host aboard the record-breaking trimaran, Groupama 3.

Le skipper de Groupama joue les hôtes à bord du trimaran batteur de records, Groupama 3.

El patrón del Groupama hace de anfitrión a bordo del trimarán rompe-récords.

弗兰科·卡玛斯向其他船长介绍破过纪录的三体帆船。

BRETAGNE IN-PORT RACE

Finally, Lorient's sailing-mad public gets a chance to see the Volvo Open 70s in action.

Les adeptes de voile lorientais peuvent enfin voir les Volvo Open 70 en action.

Un público loco por la vela finalmente pudo ver a los Volvo Open 70 en acción.

洛里昂的帆船发烧友们终于有机会亲眼目睹沃尔沃Open70大帆船比赛的风姿。

BRICE GUYART

France's Olympic champion fencer in Lorient at the invitation of Official Timekeeper, IWC Schaffhausen.

Le champion olympique français d'escrime à Lorient sur invitation du chronométreur officiel IWC Schaffhausen.

El campeón olímpico francés de esgrima en Lorient invitado por el cronometrador oficial IWC Schaffhausen

法国奥运击剑冠军应赛事官方计时IWC之邀来到洛里昂赛事村参观。

VOLVO OCEAN RACE ACADEMY

Young Optimist sailors hone their racing skills in the atmosphere of the race village.

Les jeunes régatiers en Optimist s'affutent dans l'atmosphère du village.

Jóvenes regatistas de Optimist demuestran sus habilidades de regata en el ambiente del race village.

年轻的OP级帆船选手在赛事村磨练自己的帆船技术。

GROUPAMA SAILING TEAM

Another flawless display secures in-port race honours for the hometown favourites.

Un autre sans-faute assure la victoire sur la course In-Port aux favoris locaux.

Otro despliegue de navegación perfecta les da la victoria de la in-port a los favoritos oriundos de la ciudad.

安盟保险队在洛里昂港内赛中表现堪称完美。

GURRA KRANTZ, ROBERT DAHLGREN

Volvo XC60 vs Volvo Open 70: pro skipper and pro driver accept the Land Challenge.

Volvo XC60 versus Volvo Open 70 : skipper et pilote professionnels acceptent le 'Land Challenge'.

El Volvo XC60 contra el Volvo Open 70: patrón contra piloto aceptan el Land Challenge.

沃尔沃XC60轿车和沃尔沃Open70帆船展开较量，一个在陆上，一个在海上，比拼哪方先开到高威。

Groupama sailing team had arrived
in Lorient as heroes. They departed
hoping to place their names alongside
the legends to have won sailing's most
demanding race.

Groupama sailing team est arrivé
à Lorient en héros. Ils repartent en
espérant inscrire leurs noms à côté
des légendes qui ont déjà gagné la
course la plus exigeante au monde.

Los del Groupama llegaron a
Lorient como héroes. Salieron de
allí esperando unirse a un exclusivo
grupo de ganadores de la regata más
exigente del mundo.

安盟保险队在洛里昂受到了英雄般的礼
遇，队员们也十分期待不负重望，赢得极
有分量的沃尔沃环球帆船赛总冠军。

Team Telefónica led the fleet out of Lorient, determined to recapture the sparkling form they had shown for much of the race.

Team Telefónica mène la flotte à la sortie de Lorient, déterminé à retrouver le panache du début de course.

El Telefónica lideró la flota al salir de Lorient determinado a recuperar la brillantez que había demostrado durante casi toda la regata.

西班牙电信队在绕标后率先离开洛里昂港，希望重夺昔日荣光。

It had been a race of highs and lows for Abu Dhabi. Misfortune struck again when Azzam snagged a lobster pot with the finish line in sight.

Abu Dhabi a connu des hauts et des bas. La malchance les frappe de nouveau lorsqu'Azzam, à vue de l'arrivée, se prend dans un casier de pêche.

Había sido una regata de altibajos para el Abu Dhabi Ocean Racing. La mala suerte golpea de nuevo cuando el Azzam se enganchó a una trampa para langostas con la línea de llegada a la vista.

阿布扎比队一路经历大起大落，当终点已出现在前方时，坏运气再次来袭，"阿萨姆号"挂上了捕龙虾的笼子。

Mike Sanderson was able to take advantage and score Sanya's best points-haul of the race. The team's doggedness had finally paid off.

Mike Sanderson tire avantage de la situation et offre à Sanya sa meilleure opération en termes de points. La ténacité de l'équipe paye enfin.

Mike Sanderson fue capaz de aprovechar y anotar el mejor resultado del Sanya de la regata. La perseverancia del equipo finalmente les dio resultados.

迈克·桑德森终于抓住机会，首次在离岸赛中摆脱了排名垫底的命运，一路坎坷终于在最后有了些许补偿。

Competitive to the very end: only six minutes separated the leading four boats as they rounded the iconic Fastnet Rock.

Compétitifs jusqu'au bout : six minutes seulement séparent les quatre premiers bateaux au moment de passer l'iconique rocher du Fastnet.

Competitivos hasta el final: solo seis minutos separan a los cuatro primeros barcos cuando pasaron por la mítica Fastnet Rock.

比拼一直到最后一刻：前四支船队抵达著名的法斯特奈特石的时间只相差六分钟。

First around the landmark, PUMA
again showed their class. But the
dream that had possessed Ken Read
was slipping away.

Premier à passer ce repère, PUMA
prouve une nouvelle fois son niveau.
Mais le rêve qui a possédé Ken Read
depuis Le Cap s'est échappé.

El Mar Mostro vuelve a demostrar su
clase al ser los primeros en cruzar el
faro. Pero el sueño que había poseído
a Ken Read se estaba desvaneciendo.

彪马队最先经过法斯特奈特石，但是船长
肯·里德从开普敦起就一直怀有的冠军梦
却渐行渐远了。

CAMPER overcame a startline penalty to hunt down the rest of the fleet - and now a first leg victory was in sight. Meanwhile Groupama's gaze was firmly fixed on the big prize.

CAMPER se remet d'une pénalité de départ et revient sur la flotte – sa première victoire d'étape est en vue. Groupama, lui, ne regarde que le trophée final.

El CAMPER superó una penalización en la salida y dio alcance al resto de la flota. El Groupama les dejó pasar pero su vista estaba puesta en el gran premio.

看步在出发时遭遇犯规处罚，但经过一路追赶，终于将要赢了第一个赛段胜利，而安盟保险队的心早已经交给了总冠军奖杯。

Chris Nicholson saved the best for last. After the frustration of frequent close calls, a momentous win into Galway was enough to propel CAMPER to second place overall.

Chris Nicholson garde le meilleur pour la fin. CAMPER, frustré d'être souvent passé à côté de la victoire, s'impose à Galway. C'est assez pour que l'équipage termine deuxième au général.

Chris Nicholson dejó lo mejor para el final. Tras la frustración de cuatro derrotas en etapas, una memorable victoria en Galway sirvió para impulsar al CAMPER a la segunda plaza de la general.

克里斯·尼克森把最好的表现留到了最后，在多次与冠军失之交臂后，最后赛段的获胜让看步·新西兰酋长队保住了总排名第二的位置。

Nothing could halt the French charge for the trophy. Tens of thousands of fans crowded the Galway waterfront to witness a famous victory and usher in a week-long celebration.

Rien ne peut arrêter l'assaut français sur le trophée. Des dizaines de milliers de fans envahissent le front de mer de Galway pour voir cette victoire. C'est le début d'une semaine de fête.

Nada podía detener la lucha de los franceses por el trofeo. Más de 20 000 aficionados se congregaron en Galway para ser testigos de una victoria que pasaría a los anales de la historia. Comenzaba una semana de celebraciones.

没有什么可以阻挡法国船队夺冠的步伐，数万名高威观众来到码头，目睹船队的胜利一刻，并开启长达一周的庆祝活动。

KNUT FROSTAD, TAOISEACH ENDA KENNY

The Volvo Ocean Race Trophy is delivered ahead of the speeding fleet.

Le Trophée de la Volvo Ocean Race est livré au dessus d'une flotte en pleine accélération.

El Trofeo de la Volvo Ocean Race llega antes que la rápida flota.

沃尔沃环球帆船赛冠军奖杯已经先期抵达高威。

CHRIS NICHOLSON / CAMPER, PRESIDENT MICHAEL D. HIGGINS

Delight at the race's return to Galway fills Irish hearts.

Les Irlandais ravis du retour de la course à Galway.

El entusiasmo por el regreso a Galway llena los corazones irlandeses.

赛事的回归让高威的人们充满喜悦。

TRAOLOCH COLLINS, JUAN KOUYOUMDJIAN

The designer is recognised as he celebrates a hat-trick of winners.

Le designer, auteur de trois bateaux vainqueurs, est récompensé.

El diseñador recibe un reconocimiento mientras celebra tres victorias seguidas.

"三冠王"赛船的设计者终于露出庐山真面目。

MARK 'SIDESHOW' CAMPBELL-JAMES, DOUG SPECK

Collecting the keys to a new Volvo XC60 as winner of the race's massively popular online game.

Il reçoit les clefs d'une Volvo XC60 neuve après avoir remporté le jeu en ligne de la course.

Recibiendo las llaves de un nuevo Volvo XC60 tras ganar el popular juego virtual de la regata.

在线游戏获胜者领取全新沃尔沃XC60汽车的钥匙。

OLOF PERSSON, FRANCK CAMMAS / GROUPAMA, STEFAN JACOBY

The heads of Volvo Group and Volvo Cars flank the winning skipper.

Les présidents de Volvo Group et de Volvo Cars aux côtés du skipper gagnant.

Los jefes de Volvo Group y de Volvo Cars acompañan al patrón ganador.

沃尔沃集团与沃尔沃汽车公司的两位首席执行官为冠军船队颁奖。

CASEY SMITH, KEN READ, TOM ADDIS / PUMA

Victory in the final in-port race gives PUMA the overall shortcourse title.

Une victoire sur la dernière In-Port sacre PUMA sur ces parcours courts.

La victoria en la última regata in-port le da al PUMA el título en la general de las costeras.

高威港内赛的胜利让彪马获得了港内赛系列的冠军。

PETRA HORREVOETS AND DAUGHTERS

The memory of Hans Horrevoets is honoured during the official prize-giving.

Le souvenir d'Hans Horrevoets est salué pendant la remise des prix officielle.

Homenaje a la memoria de Hans Horrevoets durante la entrega de premios oficial.

颁奖晚宴上，人们再一次缅怀在比赛中失去生命的水手汉斯。

RACE STAFF FAREWELL

Galway is also the final port-of-call for the team responsible for keeping the race going.

Galway est aussi le dernier port pour l'équipe qui assure le fonctionnement de la course.

Galway es también el último puerto responsable de mantener la regata en funcionamiento.

对于岸队来说，高威也是他们的最后一座停靠港。

The Discover Ireland In-Port Race in Galway Bay marked the end of an epic race and lowered the curtain on the Volvo Open 70 era. The Volvo Ocean Race had seen the closest, most successful edition in its rich history.

La course In-Port Discover Ireland, en baie de Galway, conclut une course épique. Le rideau tombe sur l'ère du Volvo Open 70. La Volvo Ocean Race a vécu la plus disputée et la plus réussie des éditions de son histoire.

La Discover Ireland In-Port Race en Galway marcó el fin de una mítica regata y bajó el telón de la era de los Volvo Ocean 70. La Volvo Ocean Race había disputado la más reñida y exitosa edición en su rica historia.

高威港内赛标志着本届赛事的结束以及沃尔沃Open70大帆船的谢幕，本届赛事是历史中船队实力最接近、各方面工作最成功的一届。

VOLVO OCEAN RACE
2011 - 2012
GALWAY
volvooceanrace.com
Abu Dhabi
inmarsat
VOLVO
BCG
THE BOSTON CONSULTING GROUP
DHL
The Fun Starts Here

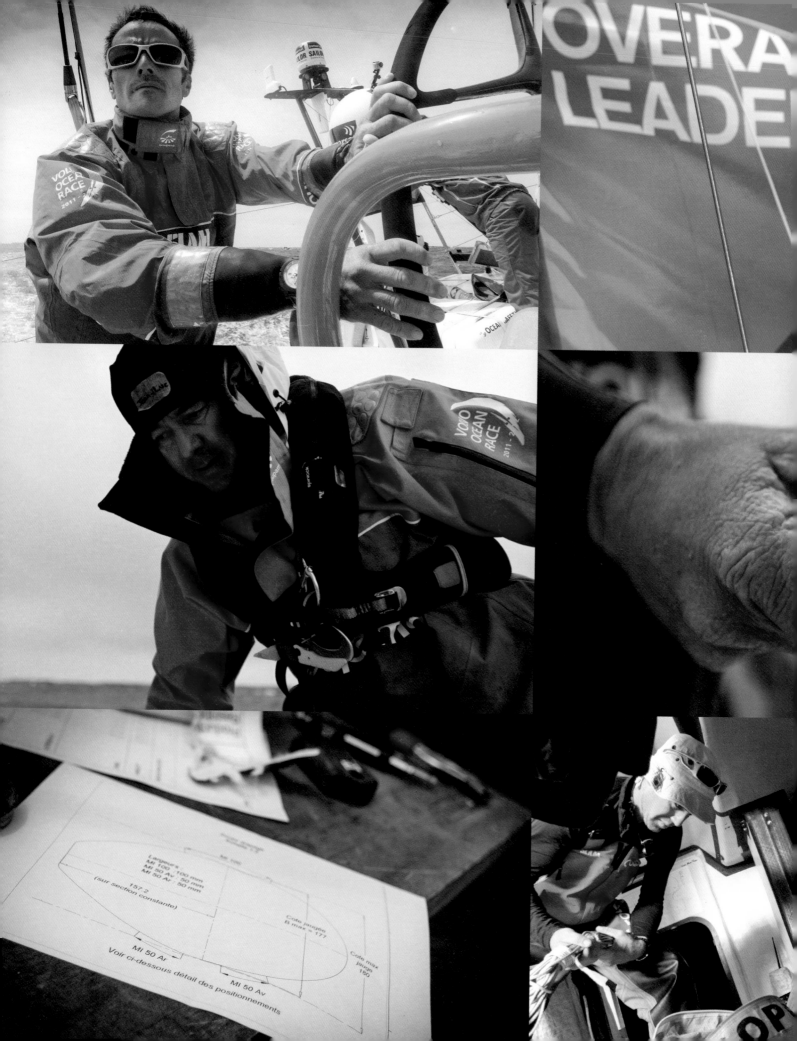

Final Standings: Overall

1 GROUPAMA SAILING TEAM (FRA)
Skipper: Franck Cammas (FRA)
Total 253 pts (Legs 212 pts / IPR 41 pts)

2 CAMPER WITH EMIRATES TEAM NZ (ESP/NZL)
Skipper: Chris Nicholson (AUS)
Total 231 pts (Legs 187 pts / IPR 44 pts)

3 PUMA OCEAN RACING POWERED BY BERG (USA)
Skipper: Ken Read (USA)
Total 226 pts (Legs 181 pts / IPR 45 pts)

4 TEAM TELEFÓNICA (ESP)
Skipper: Iker Martínez (ESP)
Total 213 pts (Legs 186 pts / IPR 27 pts)

5 ABU DHABI OCEAN RACING (UAE)
Skipper: Ian Walker (GBR)
Total 131 pts (Legs 94 pts / IPR 37 pts)

6 TEAM SANYA (CHN)
Skipper: Mike Sanderson (NZL)
Total 51 pts (Legs 35 pts / IPR 16 pts)

Final Standings: In-Port Race Series

1 PUMA OCEAN RACING POWERED BY BERG (USA)
Skipper: Ken Read (USA)
45 pts

2 CAMPER WITH EMIRATES TEAM NZ (ESP/NZL)
Skipper: Chris Nicholson (AUS)
44 pts

3 GROUPAMA SAILING TEAM (FRA)
Skipper: Ken Read (USA)
41 pts

4 ABU DHABI OCEAN RACING (UAE)
Skipper: Ian Walker (GBR)
37 pts

5 TEAM TELEFÓNICA (ESP)
Skipper: Iker Martínez (ESP)
27 pts

6 TEAM SANYA (CHN)
Skipper: Mike Sanderson (NZL)
16 pts

Race Prizes
Volvo Ocean Race 2011-12

From **Alicante**, Spain to **Galway**, Ireland. **29 October 2011–7 July 2012**. Consisting of **9 offshore legs** (total orthodromic distance: **39,270 nm**) and **10 in-port races**.

Volvo Ocean Race

Winners	**Groupama sailing team (FRA)**
Skipper	**Franck Cammas (FRA)**
Total Points	**253**
Second Place	**CAMPER with Emirates Team New Zealand (ESP/NZL)**
Skipper	**Chris Nicholson (AUS)**
Total Points	**231**
Third Place	**PUMA Ocean Racing powered by BERG (USA)**
Skipper	**Ken Read (USA)**
Total Points	**226**

In-Port Race Series

Winners	**PUMA Ocean Racing powered by BERG (USA)**
Skipper	**Ken Read (USA)**
Total Points	**45**

Abu Dhabi Seamanship Award	Brad Marsh (NZL) / Groupama sailing team (FRA)
IWC Schaffhausen Speed Record Challenge	CAMPER with Emirates Team New Zealand (ESP/NZL) Skipper: Chris Nicholson (AUS) Distance: 565.84 nm. Leg 8, 13-14 June 2012
DHL Shore Crew Award	Team Sanya (CHN) Shore Manager: Nick Bice (AUS)
Inmarsat Media Crew Member Award	Hamish Hooper (NZL) / CAMPER with Emirates Team New Zealand (ESP/NZL)
Hans Horrevoets Rookie Trophy	Dave Swete (NZL) / Team Sanya (CHN)
Ericsson Design Award	Juan Yacht Design Juan Kouyoumdjian, Principal Designer
Host Port Environmental Award	Itajaí
Roaring Forties Trophy	Groupama sailing team (FRA) Skipper: Franck Cammas (FRA)

Stage Prizes & Official Results

Iberdrola In-Port Race
Alicante, Spain
29 October 2011

1	ADOR–I. Walker	53:44	6
2	PUMA–K. Read	+14:14	5
3	CMPR–C. Nicholson	+16:27	4
4	SNYA–M. Sanderson	+16:59	3
5	GPMA–F. Cammas	+17:27	2
6	TELE–I. Martínez	+18:24	1

V&A Waterfront In-Port Race
Cape Town, South Africa
10 December 2011

1	TELE–I. Martínez	52:55	6
2	CMPR–C. Nicholson	+0:43	5
3	PUMA–K. Read	+0:52	4
4	ADOR–I. Walker	+1:19	3
5	GPMA–F. Cammas	+1:49	2
6	SNYA–M. Sanderson	+4:10	1

Etihad Airways In-Port Race
Abu Dhabi, United Arab Emirates
13 January 2012

1	ADOR–I. Walker	57:51	6
2	GPMA–F. Cammas	+0:57	5
3	CMPR–C. Nicholson	+2:56	4
4	PUMA–K. Read	+4:31	3
5	TELE–I. Martínez	+4:56	2
6	SNYA–M. Sanderson	DNS	2*

Sanya Haitang Bay In-Port Race
Sanya, China
18 February 2012

1	TELE–I. Martínez	58:37	6
2	PUMA–K. Read	+0:41	5
3	ADOR–I. Walker	+4:20	4
4	CMPR–C. Nicholson	+5:35	3
5	GPMA–F. Cammas	+6:51	2
6	SNYA–M. Sanderson	+7:13	1

Auckland In-Port Race
Auckland, New Zealand
17 March 2012

1	CMPR–C. Nicholson	1:00:38	6
2	PUMA–K. Read	+0:54	5
3	GPMA–F. Cammas	+1:26	4
4	SNYA–M. Sanderson	+2:20	3
5	ADOR–I. Walker	+2:52	2
6	TELE–I. Martínez	+3:27	1

Leg 1: Alicante-Cape Town
Distance: 6,500 nm
Start: 5 November 2011

1	TELE–I. Martínez	21d 5:14:25	30
2	CMPR–C. Nicholson	+16:33:39	25
3	GPMA–F. Cammas	+2d 23:14:06	20
–	PUMA–K. Read	DNF	0
–	ADOR–I. Walker	DNF	0
–	SNYA–M. Sanderson	DNF	0

Leg 2: Cape Town-Abu Dhabi*
Distance: 5,430 nm
Start: 11 December 2011

1	TELE–I. Martínez	29
2	CMPR–C. Nicholson	24
3	PUMA–K. Read	19
4	GPMA–F. Cammas	18
5	ADOR–I. Walker	10
6	SNYA–M. Sanderson	5

Leg 3: Abu Dhabi-Sanya*
Distance: 4,600 nm
Start: 14 January 2012

1	TELE–I. Martínez	27
2	GPMA–F. Cammas	24
3	CMPR–C. Nicholson	18
4	PUMA–K. Read	17
5	ADOR–I. Walker	14
6	SNYA–M. Sanderson	5

Leg 4: Sanya-Auckland
Distance: 5,220 nm
Start: 19 February 2012

1	GPMA–F. Cammas	19d 15:35:54	30
2	PUMA–K. Read	+12:21:56	25
3	TELE–I. Martínez	+13:09:28	20
4	CMPR–C. Nicholson	+13:11:01	15
5	ADOR–I. Walker	+13:44:41	10
6	SNYA–M. Sanderson	+14:19:49	5

Leg 5: Auckland-Itajaí
Distance: 6,705 nm
Start: 18 March 2012

1	PUMA–K. Read	19d 18:09:50	30
2	TELE–I. Martínez	+12:38	25
3	GPMA–F. Cammas	+3d 18:48:54	20
4	CMPR–C. Nicholson	+10d 17:25:53	15
-	ADOR–I. Walker	DNF	0
-	SNYA–M. Sanderson	DNF	0

Abu Dhabi Seamanship Award
Crew / Abu Dhabi Ocean Racing
IWC Schaffhausen Speed Record Challenge
CAMPER with Emirates Team New Zealand
DHL Shore Crew Award
Team Sanya
Inmarsat Media Crew Member Award
Hamish Hooper (NZL) / CAMPER with Emirates Team New Zealand

Abu Dhabi Seamanship Award
Richard Mason (NZL) & Jared Henderson (NZL) / Team Sanya
IWC Schaffhausen Speed Record Challenge
Groupama sailing team
DHL Shore Crew Award
PUMA Ocean Racing powered by BERG
Inmarsat Media Crew Member Award
Yann Riou (FRA) / Groupama sailing team

IWC Schaffhausen Speed Record Challenge
PUMA Ocean Racing powered by BERG
DHL Shore Crew Award
PUMA Ocean Racing powered by BERG
Inmarsat Media Crew Member Award
Amory Ross (USA) / PUMA Ocean Racing powered by BERG

Abu Dhabi Seamanship Award
Crew / Groupama sailing team
IWC Schaffhausen Speed Record Challenge
PUMA Ocean Racing powered by BERG
DHL Shore Crew Award
Abu Dhabi Ocean Racing
Inmarsat Media Crew Member Award
Yann Riou / Groupama sailing team

Abu Dhabi Seamanship Award
Crew / PUMA Ocean Racing powered by BERG
IWC Schaffhausen Speed Record Challenge
CAMPER with Emirates Team New Zealand
DHL Shore Crew Award
Groupama sailing team
Inmarsat Media Crew Member Award
Hamish Hooper / CAMPER with Emirates Team New Zealand

*Refer to Notes, page 181

DHL In-Port Race
Itajaí, Brazil
21 April 2012

1 GPMA-F. Cammas	46:27	6
2 CMPR-C. Nicholson	+0:48	5
3 PUMA-K. Read	+1:05	4
4 ADOR-I. Walker	+1:33	3
5 TELE-I. Martínez	+5:40	2
- SNYA-M. Sanderson	DNS	0

PORTMIAMI In-Port Race
Miami, U.S.A.
19 May 2012

1 ADOR-I. Walker	1:14:14	6
2 GPMA-F. Cammas	+0:21	5
3 PUMA-K. Read	+1:55	4
4 CMPR-C. Nicholson	+2:03	3
5 SNYA-M. Sanderson	+2:49	2
6 TELE-I. Martínez	+6:21	1

Oeiras In-Port Race
Lisbon, Portugal
9 June 2012

1 GPMA-F. Cammas	1:01:22	6
2 PUMA-K. Read	+0:22	5
3 CMPR-C. Nicholson	+1:08	4
4 ADOR-I. Walker	+1:46	3
5 SNYA-M. Sanderson	+3:28	2
6 TELE-I. Martínez	+4:17	1

Bretagne In-Port Race
Lorient, France
30 June 2012

1 GPMA-F. Cammas	56:12	6
2 CMPR-C. Nicholson	+0:13	5
3 PUMA-K. Read	+0:24	4
4 TELE-I. Martínez	+1:33	3
5 ADOR-I. Walker	+1:48	2
6 SNYA-M. Sanderson	+4:45	1

Discover Ireland In-Port Race
Galway, Ireland
7 July 2012

1 PUMA-K. Read	53:12	6
2 CMPR-C. Nicholson	+1:19	5
3 TELE-I. Martínez	+1:55	4
4 GPMA-F. Cammas	+2:29	3
5 ADOR-I. Walker	+4:00	2
6 SNYA-M. Sanderson	+4:32	1

Leg 6: Itajaí-Miami
Distance: 4,800 nm
Start: 22 April 2012

1 PUMA-K. Read	17d 1:13:59	30
2 CMPR-C. Nicholson	+1:07:25	25
3 GPMA-F. Cammas	+6:15:04	20
4 TELE-I. Martínez	+6:52:39	15
5 ADOR-I. Walker	+14:43:36	10
- SNYA-M. Sanderson	DNS	0

Leg 7: Miami-Lisbon
Distance: 3,590 nm
Start: 20 May 2012

1 ADOR-I. Walker	11d 4:23:54	30
2 GPMA-F. Cammas	+5:27	25
3 PUMA-K. Read	+2:02:58	20
4 TELE-I. Martínez	+4:04:33	15
5 CMPR-C. Nicholson	+4:06:15	10
6 SNYA-M. Sanderson	+4:20:31	5

Leg 8: Lisbon-Lorient
Distance: 1,940 nm
Start: 10 June 2012

1 GPMA-F. Cammas	4d 23:31:02	30
2 CMPR-C. Nicholson	+59:07	25
3 PUMA-K. Read	+1:12:04	20
4 ADOR-I. Walker	+2:46:23	15
5 TELE-I. Martínez	+9:09:24	10
6 SNYA-M. Sanderson	+9:28:39	5

Leg 9: Lorient-Galway
Distance: 485 nm
Start: 1 July 2012

1 CMPR-C. Nicholson	1d 13:40:13	30
2 GPMA-F. Cammas	+6:58	25
3 PUMA-K. Read	+12:48	20
4 TELE-I. Martínez	+17:20	15
5 SNYA-M. Sanderson	+2:32:14	10
6 ADOR-I. Walker	+2:41:16	5

IWC Schaffhausen Speed Record Challenge
PUMA Ocean Racing powered by BERG
DHL Shore Crew Award
Abu Dhabi Ocean Racing
Inmarsat Media Crew Member Award
Amory Ross / PUMA Ocean Racing powered by BERG

Abu Dhabi Seamanship Award
Jono Swain (RSA) / PUMA Ocean Racing
powered by BERG
IWC Schaffhausen Speed Record Challenge
Groupama sailing team
DHL Shore Crew Award
CAMPER with Emirates Team New Zealand
Inmarsat Media Crew Member Award
Nick Dana (USA) / Abu Dhabi Ocean Racing

Abu Dhabi Seamanship Award
Brad Marsh (NZL) / Groupama sailing team
IWC Schaffhausen Speed Record Challenge
CAMPER with Emirates Team New Zealand
DHL Shore Crew Award
Team Sanya
Inmarsat Media Crew Member Award
Hamish Hooper / CAMPER with Emirates
Team New Zealand

IWC Schaffhausen Speed Record Challenge
PUMA Ocean Racing powered by BERG
Inmarsat Media Crew Member Award
Yann Riou / Groupama sailing team

Crew Lists 2011-12

Team	Name	Nat	Role	In-Port Races 1-10	Legs 1-9
Abu Dhabi Ocean Racing (UAE)	Ian Walker	GBR	Skipper	• • • • • • • • • •	• • • • • • • • •
	Nick Dana	USA	Media Crew Member	• • • • • • • • • •	• • • • • • • • •
	Justin Ferris	NZL	Helmsman/Trimmer	• • • • ○ ○ ○ ○ ○ ○	• • • ○ ○ ○ ○ ○ ○
	Simon Fisher	GBR	Helmsman/Trimmer	• • • • • • • • • •	• • • • • • • • •
	Rob Greenhalgh	GBR	Watch Leader	• • • • • • • • • •	• • • • • • • • •
	Adil Khalid	UAE	Helmsman/Trimmer	• • • • • • • • • •	• • • • • • • • •
	Andrew Lewis	USA	Helmsman/Trimmer	○ • • ○ ○ ○ ○ ○ ○ ○	• ○ ○ ○ ○ ○ ○ ○ ○
	Wade Morgan	AUS	Bowman	• • • • • • • • • •	• • • • • • • • •
	Anthony Nossiter	AUS	Helmsman/Trimmer	○ ○ ○ ○ ○ •	○ ○ ○ ○ •
	Jules Salter	GBR	Navigator	• • • • • • • • • •	• • • • • • • • •
	Craig Satterthwaite	NZL	Watch Leader	• • • • • • • • • •	• • • • • • • • •
	Justin Slattery	IRL	Bowman	• • • • • • • • • •	• • • • • • • • •
	Paul Willcox	RSA	Helmsman/Trimmer	• ○ ○	○ ○ ○
CAMPER with Emirates Team New Zealand (ESP/NZL)	Chris Nicholson	AUS	Skipper	• • • • • • • • • •	• • • • • • • • •
	Stu Bannatyne	NZL	Co-Skipper/Watch Captain	• • • • • • • • • •	• • • • • • • • •
	'Chuny' Bermúdez	ESP	Helmsman/Trimmer	• • • • • • • • • •	• • • • • • • • •
	Nick Burridge	NZL	Bowman	○ ○ ○ ○ ○ ○ • ○	○ ○ ○ ○ ○ • ○
	Hamish Hooper	NZL	Media Crew Member	• • • • • • • • • •	• • • • • • • • •
	Andrew McLean	NZL	Pitman/Trimmer	• • • • • • • • • •	• • • • • • • • •
	Adam Minoprio	NZL	Helmsman/Trimmer	• • • • • • • • • •	• • • • • • • • •
	Will Oxley	AUS	Navigator	• • • • • • • • • •	• • • • • • • • •
	Mike Pammenter	RSA	Bowman/Boat Captain	• • • • • ○ ○ ○ • ○	○ ○ ○
	Tony Rae	NZL	Helmsman/Trimmer	• • • • • • • • • •	• • • • • • • • •
	Rob Salthouse	NZL	Helmsman/Trimmer	• • • • • • • • • •	• • • • • • • • •
	Daryl Wislang	NZL	Bowman	• • • • • • • • • •	• • • • • • • • •
Groupama sailing team (FRA)	Franck Cammas	FRA	Skipper	• • • • • • • • • •	• • • • • • • • •
	Charles Caudrelier	FRA	Helmsman/Trimmer	• • • • • • • • • •	• • • • • • • • •
	Thomas Coville	FRA	Helmsman/Trimmer	• • • • • • • • • •	• • • • • • • • •
	Damian Foxall	IRL	Helmsman/Trimmer	• • • • • • • • • •	• • • • • • • • •
	Phil Harmer	AUS	Helmsman/Trimmer	• • • • • • • • • •	• • • • • • ○ • •
	Erwan Israël	FRA	Trimmer/Helmsman	• • • • • • • • • •	• • ○ • • ○ • • •
	Martin Krite	SWE	Bowman/Boat Captain	• • • • • • • • • •	• • • • • • • • •
	Brad Marsh	NZL	Bowman	• • • • • • • • • •	• • • • • • • • •
	Jean-Luc Nélias	FRA	Navigator	○ ○ • • • ○ ○ ○ ○ ○	• • • • • • • • ○
	Laurent Pagès	FRA	Trimmer/Helmsman	• • ○ ○ ○ • •	• ○ ○ • • • • •
	Yann Riou	FRA	Media Crew Member	• • • • • • • • • •	• • • • • • • • •
	Martin Strömberg	SWE	Helmsman/Trimmer/Pitman	• • • • • • • • • •	• • • • • • • • •
PUMA Ocean Racing powered by BERG (USA)	Ken Read	USA	Skipper	• • • • • • • • • •	• • • • • • • • •
	Tom Addis	AUS	Navigator	• • • • • • • • • •	• • • • • • • • •
	Shannon Falcone	ANT	Bowman	○ ○ ○ ○ ○ • ○ ○ ○	○ ○ ○ ○ ○ • ○ ○ ○
	Ryan Godfrey	AUS	Helmsman/Trimmer	• • • • • • • • • •	• • • • • • • • •
	Kelvin Harrap	NZL	Helmsman/Trimmer	• • • • • • • • • •	• • • • • ○ • • •
	Brad Jackson	NZL	Watch Leader	• • • • • • • • • •	• • • • • • • • •
	Thomas Johanson	FIN	Helmsman/Trimmer	○ ○ ○ • ○ ○ ○ ○ ○ ○	• • ○ • • • • • •
	Rome Kirby	USA	Helmsman/Trimmer	• • • • • • • • • •	• • • • • • • • •
	Michi Müller	GER	Bowman	• • • • • • • • • •	• • • • • • • • •
	Tony Mutter	NZL	Watch Leader	• • • • • • • • • •	• • • • • • • • •
	Amory Ross	USA	Media Crew Member	• • • • • • • • • •	• • • • • • • • •
	Casey Smith	AUS	Bowman	• • • • • ○ • • • •	○ • • • • • • •
	Jono Swain	RSA	Helmsman/Trimmer	• • • • • • • • • •	• • • • • • • • •
Team Sanya (CHN)	Mike Sanderson	NZL	Skipper	• • ○ • • • • • •	• • • • • • • • •
	Cameron Dunn	NZL	Watch Captain	• • ○ • • • • • •	• • • • • • • • •
	Jared Henderson	NZL	Bowman/Trimmer	• • ○ • ○ • ○ • ○	• ○ • ○ • ○ • ○
	Ryan Houston	NZL	Helmsman/Trimmer	• • ○ • • • • • •	• • • • • • • • •
	Teng Jiang He 'Tiger'	CHN	Trimmer/Grinder	• • ○ • • • • • •	• • • • • • • • •
	Martin Kirketerp	DEN	Helmsman/Trimmer	○ ○ ○ • ○ • • • •	○ ○ ○ • • • • •
	Aksel Magdahl	NOR	Navigator	• • ○ • • • • • •	• • • • • • • • •
	Chris Main	NZL	Watch Leader	• ○ ○ ○ ○ ○ ○ ○ ○	• ○ ○ ○ ○ ○ ○ ○ ○
	Richard Mason	NZL	Helmsman/Trimmer	• • ○ • • • • • •	• • • • • • • • •
	Andy Meiklejohn	NZL	Bowman/Boat Captain	• • ○ • ○ ○ ○ ○ ○	• ○ ○ ○ ○ ○ ○ ○
	David Rolfe	NZL	Helmsman/Trimmer	• • ○ • ○ • ○ • ○	• ○ • ○ • ○ • ○
	Bert Schandevyl	BEL	Bowman	• • ○ • • • • • •	• • • • • • • • •
	Andrés Soriano	ESP	Media Crew Member	• • ○ • • • • • •	• • • • • • • • •
	Dave Swete	NZL	Helmsman/Trimmer	• • ○ • • • ○	• • • • • • ○
Team Telefónica (ESP)	Iker Martínez	ESP	Skipper	• • • • • • • • • •	• • • • • • • • •
	Pablo Arrarte	ESP	Helmsman/Trimmer	• • • • • • • • • •	• • • • • • • • •
	Jordi Calafat	ESP	Helmsman/Sail Co-ordinator	• • • • • • • • • •	• • • • • • • • •
	Andrew Cape	AUS	Navigator	• • • • • • • • • •	• • • • • • • • •
	'Ñeti' Cuervas-Mons	ESP	Bowman	• • • • • • • • • •	• • • • • • • • •
	Xabi Fernández	ESP	Helmsman/Trimmer	• • • • • • • • • •	• • • • • • • • •
	Diego Fructuoso	ESP	Media Crew Member	• • • • • • • • • •	• • • • • • • • •
	Zane Gills	AUS	Bowman	• • • • • • • • • •	• • • • • • • • •
	Iñigo Losada	ESP	Helmsman/Trimmer	○ ○ ○ ○ ○ ○ ○ • ○	○ ○ ○ ○ ○ ○ ○ ○
	Neal McDonald	GBR	Watch Leader	• • • • • • • • • •	• • • • • • • • •
	Pepe Ribes	ESP	Boat Captain	• • • • • • • • • •	• • • • • • • • •
	'Joca' Signorini	BRA	Watch Leader	• • • • • • • • • •	• • • • • • • • •

Leg 2: Cape Town–Abu Dhabi

Due to anti-piracy measures, Leg 2 points were scored by adding the points won on each of two scoring stages. Official times were recorded in respect of each scoring stage:

Stage 1: Cape Town–Malé
Start: 11 December 2011

1 TELE–I. Martínez	15d 4:57:19	24
2 CMPR–C. Nicholson	+1:57	20
3 PUMA–K. Read	+5:35:50	16
4 GPMA–F. Cammas	+8:07:00	12
5 ADOR–I. Walker	+14:59:18	8
6 SNYA–M. Sanderson	+24d 1:05:56	4

Stage 2: Sharjah–Abu Dhabi
Start: 4 January 2012

1 GPMA–F. Cammas	6:52:09	6
2 TELE–I. Martínez	+0:52	5
3 CMPR–C. Nicholson	+5:41	4
4 PUMA–K. Read	+6:31	3
5 ADOR–I. Walker	+10:12	2
6 SNYA–M. Sanderson	DNS	1*

Points awarded due to Team Sanya completing Leg 2–Stage 1 in racing conditions

Etihad Airways In-Port Race

Points awarded due to Team Sanya completing Leg 2-Stage 1 in racing conditions.

Leg 3: Abu Dhabi–Sanya

Due to anti-piracy measures, Leg 3 points were scored by adding the points won on each of two scoring stages. Official times were recorded in respect of each scoring stage:

Stage 1: Abu Dhabi–Sharjah
Start: 14 January 2012

1 ADOR–I. Walker	6:29:45	6
2 PUMA–K. Read	+1:16	5
3 GPMA–F. Cammas	+3:24	4
4 TELE–I. Martínez	+5:00	3
5 CMPR–C. Nicholson	+8:49	2
6 SNYA–M. Sanderson	DNS	1*

Stage 2: Malé–Sanya
Start: 22 January 2012

1 TELE–I. Martínez	12d 19:58:21	24
2 GPMA–F. Cammas	+1:47:03	20
3 CMPR–C. Nicholson	+3:30:02	16
4 PUMA–K. Read	+4:30:51	12
5 ADOR–I. Walker	+7:06:44	8
6 SNYA–M. Sanderson	+1d 8:36:55	4

Points awarded due to Team Sanya completing Leg 2–Stage 1 in racing conditions

Key to Abbreviations

ADOR ABU DHABI OCEAN RACING / **CMPR** CAMPER WITH EMIRATES TEAM NEW ZEALAND / **GPMA** GROUPAMA SAILING TEAM / **PUMA** PUMA OCEAN RACING POWERED BY BERG / **SNYA** TEAM SANYA / **TELE** TEAM TELEFÓNICA

TRANSLATED TEXTS

16 Plus que l'ouverture de la plus épique des courses au large, les premiers 6500 milles de la Volvo Ocean Race 2011-12 doivent surtout donner une idée de l'épreuve à venir. Depuis 1997-98, depuis qu'une seule classe dispute la course, le vainqueur de la première étape a toujours été le vainqueur final. De quoi faire de cette descente d'Alicante au Cap un moment crucial.

En novembre 2011, cinq des six équipages présents sur la Costa Blanca espagnole pour la première étape peuvent rêver de gloire à Galway. Team Sanya et son bateau de la génération précédente sont les seuls vrais outsiders. Sur les pontons, les experts affirment que la course se jouera sur des détails.

Une promesse logique, mais c'était sans compter sur l'imprévisibilité de la nature. Dès le départ de l'étape 1, les extrêmes éclipsent ces détails. Le champ de course le plus dur au monde ne tarde pas à nous rappeler son invincibilité. Même la Méditerranée, habituellement plus soumise, semble vouloir traiter avec mépris les préparations et investissements les plus minutieux.

À terre aussi la course exige aussi beaucoup des équipes techniques, de la direction de course et des équipes logistiques et médiatiques, qui s'efforcent de faire face aux évènements sur l'eau. Les amis et familles des marins savent que le triomphalisme aura peu de place avant l'arrivée de tous, sains et saufs, à Galway.

À la fois excitante et terrifiante, la course frôle de nouveau l'extrême. Elle va devenir une obsession pour les 66 marins – et pour le reste d'entre nous – pendant les huit prochains mois.

38 La course a affronté de nombreux dangers tout au long de son histoire. Mais le parcours 2011-12 présente des risques bien différents. Avec un total de 237 attaques, kidnappings et autres incidents au large de la côte est africaine en 2011, la piraterie est le danger numéro un pour les semaines à venir.

Assurer la sécurité des équipages dans l'océan Indien, et ce bien avant Abu Dhabi, est l'opération logistique la plus complexe jamais entreprise par la course.

C'est Le Cap – port d'accueil pour la huitième fois, un chiffre record – qui salue la flotte au départ des 5430 milles d'une étape divisée en deux.

Les informations à l'approche de l'arrivée de la première partie de l'étape doivent être gardées secrètes. Dans la zone furtive, Telefónica et CAMPER se disputent la part du lion en duel.

Une fois dans le port secret, les bateaux sont chargés à bord d'un cargo pour transiter jusqu'au large de Sharjah, au nord des Emirats. À partir de là, restent 98 milles de sprint pour rejoindre les eaux scintillantes et l'accueil chaleureux d'Abu Dhabi.

Soigneusement organisée, l'opération évite un véritable danger aux athlètes et à leurs bateaux. Elle rappelle aussi au public les risques pris par les marins.

52 "Travellers Welcome". Jamais le slogan d'Abu Dhabi n'a été plus approprié. Une réception chaleureuse salue la première incursion de la course dans les eaux arabes. Le 4 janvier 2012, la course au large touche un nouveau coin de la planète, ouvrant ses portes à de nouvelles affinités dans le monde du sport.

Quelques jours plus tôt, 25 000 fans étaient présents sur le village et sur le port pour célébrer le Nouvel An et le concert du groupe britannique Coldplay – le premier des nombreux moments magiques à suivre.

Le sprint le long de la côte émirienne offre aux locaux une introduction électrifiante à la course au large. Plus de 120 000 spectateurs passent les portes du village de la course pour en expérimenter l'atmosphère. Ils viennent surtout pour Azzam et Adil. Azzam – le bateau local qui porte le nom arabe pour « détermination ». Adil Kalid – l'équipier émirien qui personnifie cette valeur au nom de sa nation.

C'est l'occasion pour les équipes de se reposer en famille et de prendre les vacances dont on manque en mer. Des problèmes de gréement sur l'étape 2 empêchent toutefois Sanya de se trouver parmi eux. Ils sont en train de se frayer un chemin au travers de conditions et de routes maritimes hasardeuses pour essayer de rejoindre la course.

68 Une tendance se dessine alors qu'une foule de touristes envahit la Serenity Marina de Sanya. Les performances irréprochables de Telefónica forcent le reste de la flotte à se remettre en question. La pression monte, il faut stopper cette charge espagnole.

Quatre équipages ont jusqu'ici partagé les podiums des étapes de large mais la régularité du bateau bleu a permis à Telefónica de creuser une avance significative. La mi-course approche et il reste beaucoup de points à prendre. PUMA, CAMPER et Groupama savent l'importance de l'étape 4. C'est maintenant ou jamais qu'il faut s'imposer comme un candidat véritablement apte à remporter la victoire.

Iker Martínez et Xabi Fernández n'ont pas ce souci. Leurs adversaires coincés, les récents Marins du Monde de l'Année rentrent s'entraîner en Espagne avant leur nouvelle tentative d'or olympique en 49er aux Jeux Olympiques de Londres.

Des conditions hostiles en mer de Chine du sud ouvrent 20 jours d'une navigation punitive. Les moments clefs de l'étape 4 montrent aussi l'évolution de la voile professionnelle, avec une compétition d'un nouveau niveau qui réduit à rien les écarts entre première et dernière places.

84 Depuis le début de la course en 1973, les étapes des mers du sud ont acquis un statut quasi mythique. Les puristes y voient une épreuve pour les vrais marins et, pour tous, le passage du Cap Horn est un rituel.

Mais c'est plus que du prestige que la flotte va chercher dans le Pacifique. Il y a l'attrait de la première place et de ses 30 points, et entre le chaleureux village de la course à Auckland et Itajaí, 6705 milles plus loin, au Brésil, les équipages vont souffrir du manque de confort implacable des 40e rugissants et des 50e hurlants. Une limite de parcours placée par 58° sud éloigne la flotte des dangers des glaces.

Les événements à suivre resteront à la fois parmi les meilleurs et les pires de cette édition. Jour après jour, les bateaux rapportent des avaries dues aux conditions difficiles. Toutes les équipes – sauf une – devront s'arrêter pour effectuer des réparations et seules quatre d'entre elles atteindront la ligne d'arrivée. L'accueil des marins par des milliers de fans à Itajaí conclut une étape inexorablement dramatique. Une étape que le reste d'entre nous avons seulement pu suivre en nous demandant comment une telle vie était possible.

106

Après les drames de l'étape 5, le souffle d'Itajaí est une thérapie. Seul Sanya, blessé, est en route en cargo pour rejoindre la course à Miami. Les autres équipes tirent le maximum de cette escale brésilienne pour réparer et se reposer.

La mainmise de Telefónica sur le large avait été stoppée un mois auparavant par Groupama. Cette fois, c'est PUMA qui a montré que le bateau bleu pouvait être mangé. Pas de quoi sous-estimer Telefónica non plus. Leur course-poursuite sur les 1500 dernières milles vers Itajaí l'a prouvé : seul PUMA les a de justesse empêchés de prendre une victoire soi-disant impossible.

En théorie, les 20 points d'avance de Martínez et de son équipage leur laissent le choix : naviguer à fond ou contrôler leurs concurrents. En réalité, leurs rivaux sont bien trop bons et ont trop confiance en leur bateau pour se laisser dicter leurs choix. Leurs trois poursuivants directs trépignent et les leaders de la course commencent à faire des erreurs.

En 17 jours, l'étape 6 va retourner le classement, éclairant la course d'un jour nouveau. Déjà la plus longue et peut-être la plus dure de l'histoire de la Volvo Ocean Race, l'édition 2011-12 devient aussi la plus serrée jamais disputée.

122

En novembre 2011, la flotte avait quitté l'Espagne à armes égales et l'arrivée semblait bien loin. Six mois plus tard, la course revient sur la péninsule ibérique et rien ne sépare les quatre premiers. Le final s'annonce haletant et quitter Miami est, pour les principaux concurrents, un nouveau départ.

La course est ouverte mais la marge d'erreur diminue à vue d'œil. Les points gagnés sont aussi des points pris aux rivaux et plusieurs duels peuvent désormais modifier le classement.

Personne ne peut non plus se permettre les avaries couteuses de la première moitié de course. À partir de maintenant, un petit recul momentané peut affecter toute une campagne. La vigilance des équipiers est plus que jamais mise à l'épreuve, surtout avec des skippers sur qui la pression de marquer des points est de plus en plus forte.

L'avance de Telefónica s'embrume tandis que les forces de la nature menacent la côte de la Floride. La tempête tropicale Alberto ne prend pas en compte la complexité de la course et ajoute un facteur de risque au retour de la flotte vers l'Europe.

140

Ville au riche héritage maritime, Lisbonne est l'escale légitime d'une épreuve prête à marquer l'histoire. En quatre décennies, la première des courses au large a souvent vécu des drames, mais jamais la compétition n'avait atteint un tel niveau.

Fascinante pour plusieurs raisons, l'étape 8 promet, entre autres, un duel spécial entre Groupama et Telefónica. Trois points seulement séparent les deux équipes qui retournent en un endroit du monde qu'elles regardent comme leur pré carré. Chacun sait qu'une seule erreur peut effacer en un instant des années de préparation. Sans oublier le risque d'être balayé par PUMA et CAMPER ou d'être mis hors concours par le golfe de Gascogne.

Sur le papier, l'étape 8 semble facile : 1940 milles avec pas plus de deux manœuvres majeures à effectuer pour les équipes. Mais en mer, les conditions sont bien moins simples. Tactiques et sens marins sont nécessaires.

Pour le marin professionnel moderne, elle s'annonce comme une vraie épreuve. Tout est en jeu et seule la puissance brute des Volvo Open 70 permettra de se battre : pas de place pour les craintifs.

La flotte se courbe sous la pression ambiante et la tension remplit le village de la course à Lisbonne. Dans un peu moins de cinq jours, un autre drame va se jouer, un qui pourrait rester dans les mémoires pour 40 autres années.

154

Pour toute une flotte de marins fatigués, huit mois de course à l'extrême arrivent à terme. Depuis la toute première nuit, les conditions difficiles ont régulièrement soumis les bateaux et les hommes à d'énormes contraintes. La tempête à l'approche de Lorient a encore rappelé l'étendue du challenge auquel ces équipages font face sur les bateaux actuels.

La météo et l'état de la mer ont laissé leurs traces, mais la 11e édition de la Volvo Ocean Race s'est surtout distinguée par l'esprit de compétition des marins eux-mêmes. Un pur désir de victoire a fait de la plus longue des courses une épreuve exigeante mentalement et physiquement.

Sur le village de la course à Lorient, beaucoup de public, et un public bruyant. Fans de voile, ils sont venus saluer les équipages et soutenir leurs héros locaux. Franck Cammas et ses hommes ont choisi de se battre contre les meilleurs et, à une étape de la fin, ils sont sur le point de gagner la Volvo Ocean Race.

S'ils arrivent à Galway dans les quatre premiers, ce sera suffisant pour leur assurer la victoire. Derrière eux, une formidable bagarre attend PUMA, CAMPER et Telefónica, que seulement six points séparent. Leur rêve de victoire finale vacille, mais la peur de perdre leur place sur le podium, elle, est bien réelle. De la gloire à l'échec, l'écart n'a jamais été aussi faible.

16 Además de ser los compases iniciales de la épica vuelta al mundo, las primeras 6500 millas de la Volvo Ocean Race 2011-12 aportarían importantes pistas de lo que iba a ser la competición entera. Desde que la regata comenzó a disputarse en una sola clase de barcos, en 1997-98, el ganador de la primera etapa había ganado la general, convirtiendo el largo y arduo camino hacia el sur, desde Alicante a Ciudad del Cabo, en un punto de referencia fundamental.

Cinco de los seis equipos que salieron de la Costa Blanca para la etapa inicial en noviembre de 2011 tenían razones para soñar con la gloria en Galway, siendo el Team Sanya el único con pocas posibilidades debido a su barco de la anterior generación. Para los expertos, ganar o perder sería cuestión de matices.

Si eso era lo que nos decía la lógica, se le olvidó decírselo a la naturaleza. Los matices se fueron por la borda cuando los extremos definieron la Etapa 1 desde el principio. El recorrido no perdió el tiempo en recordarnos que es indomable. Incluso el normalmente sumiso Mediterráneo trató con desprecio a la meticulosa preparación de los equipos.

La regata también exigió un alto precio a los equipos de tierra, de control, de logística y de comunicación que tuvieron que responder inmediatamente a los acontecimientos. Amigos y familiares de los regatistas sabían que no podrían dormir tranquilos hasta que los equipos llegaran sanos y salvos a Galway.

Fue emocionante y aterrador al mismo tiempo. La vida al extremo volvía a estar de moda y se convertiría en una obsesión para 66 regatistas –y para el resto de nosotros– durante los siguientes ocho meses.

38 A través de su fascinante historia, la regata se ha enfrentado a todo tipo de peligros. Pero añadir una escala en el golfo Pérsico implicó una serie de riesgos absolutamente nuevos. Un total de 237 ataques, secuestros y otros incidentes en la costa del Este de África en 2011 significaba que la piratería sería el principal peligro al que la flota se iba a enfrentar en las semanas siguientes.

Garantizar la seguridad de las tripulaciones en el océano Índico, mucho antes de alcanzar Abu Dabi, iba a demandar la operación logística más compleja que la regata jamás había llevado a cabo.

Ciudad del Cabo –anfitriona de la regata por octava vez, todo un récord– se despidió de una flota que comenzaba una etapa de 5430 millas náuticas dividida en dos partes puntuables.

La información sobre la aproximación de la flota a la llegada de la primera parte se mantuvo en secreto. En condiciones de modo invisible –sin desvelar su localización– el Telefónica se enzarzó en una feroz lucha con el CAMPER por los puntos de la etapa.

Una vez en puerto seguro, se cargaron los barcos en un mercante para llevarlos, bajo escolta armada, a una posición en la costa de Sharjah, en los Emiratos del norte. Desde aquí, un esprín final de 98 millas náuticas hasta las aguas cristalinas de Abu Dabi y su calurosa bienvenida.

Una operación meticulosamente planeada evitó a los regatistas y sus barcos un serio peligro, a la vez que sirvió de recordatorio gráfico a los espectadores de la adversidad y los graves riesgos a los que se enfrentan los marineros.

52 "Bienvenidos viajeros." El eslogan de Abu Dabi no podía ser más adecuado. La más calurosa bienvenida sirvió para anunciar la primera incursión de la regata en aguas del golfo Pérsico. El 4 de enero de 2012 marcó el momento en que las regatas de altura llegaron a otra esquina del mundo, abriendo camino a nuevas amistades en la aldea global de este deporte.

Sólo unos días antes, 25 000 aficionados inundaron el race village y la marina para recibir el año nuevo con un concierto del grupo roquero británico Coldplay. Fue la inauguración de un lugar que albergaría muchos más momentos mágicos en los días venideros.

Un arrollador esprín por la costa emiratí ofreció a los presentes una apasionante introducción a la vela de alto rendimiento. Más de 120 000 espectadores vinieron a saborear el ambiente del race village. Sobre todo, vinieron por el Azzam y por Adil. El Azzam –el barco emiratí que significa "determinación" en árabe– y Adil Khadil, el regatista nativo que personifica ese atributo en representación de la nación.

Para los equipos, ésta era una oportunidad de relajarse con la familia y disfrutar de unas merecidas vacaciones. Los problemas de aparejo que sufrió en la Etapa 2 el Team Sanya hicieron imposible que estuviera entre ellos. Su oportunidad de reincorporarse a la regata llegó entre un laberinto de condiciones inestables y rutas de mercantes rumbo a su puerto base.

68 Una secuencia de actuaciones impecables del Telefónica obligó al resto de la flota a analizar su propio rendimiento. Mientras el numeroso público abarrotaba la Serenity Marina de Sanya, la presión subía entre los equipos para detener la ofensiva de los españoles para conseguir el trofeo.

Cuatro equipos habían ocupado las posiciones de podio en la regata hasta ahora, pero la impresionante consistencia del equipo azul les estaba ayudando a crear una sólida ventaja sobre sus rivales. Con el ecuador de la regata aproximándose, aún quedaban muchos puntos en juego. Pero las mentes detrás del PUMA, el CAMPER y el Groupama sabían que la Etapa 4 iba a ser decisiva. Para ellos, se trataba de ahora o nunca si querían mantener alguna posibilidad de ganar.

Iker Martínez y Xabi Fernández no tenían que pensar en eso. Mientras que sus rivales se inquietaban, los recién coronados Mejores Regatistas del Mundo en 2011 regresaban a España para sumar unas valiosas horas de entrenamiento en su conquista del oro olímpico en la clase 49er.

Las condiciones hostiles en el mar de China Meridional reinaron durante veinte días de dura navegación.

La apretadísima llegada de la Etapa 4 demostraría la magnitud de la transformación que había tenido lugar en el mundo de la vela profesional. Nuevos niveles de competitividad han revolucionado el deporte, produciendo márgenes infinitesimales entre el primero y el último.

84 Desde la primera edición en 1973, las etapas en el océano Antártico siempre han tenido un estatus especial, casi mítico. Los puristas las consideran como la única prueba verdadera para un regatista y rodear el cabo de Hornos es un rito iniciático para todos.

Pero había mucho más que prestigio en juego cuando la flota puso rumbo al vasto Pacífico. La primera posición y 30 puntos estaban en juego, pero entre la calidez del race village e Itajaí en Brasil, a 6705 millas náuticas, las tripulaciones iban a aguantar despiadadas fatigas al atravesar los Cuarenta Rugientes y los Furiosos Cincuenta. Se puso un límite al recorrido del 58º Sur para quitar el hielo y las velocidades temerarias de la lista de peligros que aguardaban a la flota.

Los acontecimientos que sucedieron tuvieron momentos gloriosos y momentos terribles. Día tras día, los informes llegaban de barcos sufriendo roturas en manos de condiciones extremas. Todos menos un equipo tuvieron que parar para llevar a cabo reparaciones en algún momento dado y solo cuatro cruzarían la línea de llegada. Las miles de personas en Itajaí dándoles la bienvenida a los barcos fue la culminación de una etapa implacable y espectacular. El resto de nosotros solo podíamos mirar y maravillarnos de cómo debe ser vivir así.

106 Tras la intensidad de la Etapa 5, el ambiente distendido de Itajaí fue una absoluta terapia. Mientras que el siniestrado Sanya zarpaba –subido a un carguero desde Nueva Zelanda– para reincorporarse a la regata en Miami, los otros equipos emplearon la escala brasileña para recuperarse, reagruparse y hacer balance de la regata.

El dominio del Telefónica en las etapas ya lo había roto el Groupama hacía un mes y ahora el PUMA también había demostrado que el barco azul no era invencible. Sin embargo nadie podía decir que el Telefónica estaba derrotado. Una persecución implacable al Mar Mostro durante las últimas 1500 millas náuticas hasta Itajaí demostró su clase una vez más, aunque el PUMA les negara por poco una victoria casi imposible.

En teoría, una ventaja de 20 puntos en lo alto de la tabla les daba a Iker Martínez y su tripulación el lujo de elegir entre navegar a tope hasta el final o mantener el ritmo de sus rivales. Pero la realidad era que sus rivales estaban alejándose demasiado rápido y con la suficiente confianza en sus barcos como para dejar que les marcasen el ritmo. Los tres equipos perseguidores estaban acercándose y los líderes de la regata comenzaban a cometer errores.

En 17 días, la Etapa 6 iba a alterar el orden establecido de lo alto de la clasificación y darle un enfoque totalmente diferente

a la regata. La que ya era la más larga y quizás la más dura edición en la historia de la Volvo Ocean Race, la edición 2011-12, se había convertido rápidamente en la más reñida.

122 En noviembre de 2011, la flota salió de España en igualdad de condiciones y con la línea de llegada a un mundo de distancia. Seis meses más tarde, la regata regresaba a la península Ibérica con pocos puntos de separación entre los cuatro primeros equipos. Para los principales competidores, la salida de Miami era como si pusieran el marcador a cero y comenzaran la regata de nuevo.

Aunque el resultado de la regata estaba totalmente abierto, el margen de error estaba reduciéndose a velocidades desorbitadas. Cada punto obtenido era un punto menos que sumaban los rivales y a partir de ahora varios duelos en la flota tenían potencial de rehacer la clasificación.

Estaba claro que nadie podía permitirse repetir los problemas que habían resultado tan costosos en la primera mitad de la regata. De ahora en adelante, incluso un contratiempo menor tenía el poder de infligir un daño irreparable en una campaña entera. Más que nunca, se requería que las tripulaciones estuvieran alertas, especialmente con los patrones sobrellevando la creciente presión de aprovechar cualquier oportunidad de asegurar unos valiosos puntos.

El liderato del Telefónica se tambaleaba mientras la fuerza de la naturaleza conspiraba en la costa de Florida. La tormenta tropical Alberto demostró un total desprecio por las dificultades que ya tenían los equipos y añadió una escalofriante dimensión al potencial retorno de la flota a Europa.

140 La Etapa 8 fue intensa por diferentes razones, pero la perspectiva de un duelo entre el Groupama y el Telefónica le dio aún más emoción. Solo tres puntos separaban a los dos equipos que navegaban rumbo a un continente que ambos consideraban como su hogar. Cada uno sabía que un solo error podía destruir años de preparación en un instante. El riesgo añadido de ser destronados por el PUMA o el CAMPER, o arrastrados fuera de combate por el despiadado golfo de Vizcaya, contribuía a la intriga.

Sobre el papel, la Etapa 8 parecía muy simple: el recorrido de 1940 millas náuticas exigía solo dos maniobras importantes de los equipos. Pero ya en el mar, las condiciones eran considerablemente menos claras. Se requería una táctica de primera y un impecable saber hacer marinero.

Se trataba de una prueba de fuego para cualquier regatista profesional de hoy en día. Con todo aún en juego y solo la fuerza bruta de un Volvo Open 70 para conseguirlo, no había lugar para cobardes.

Mientras la flota se preparaba para una travesía de alto riesgo, la tensión crecía en el race village de Lisboa. En poco menos de cinco días, se iba representar otro drama en la saga de la regata, un drama que podría perdurar en el recuerdo otros 40 años.

154

Para la flota de hombres agotados, los ocho meses de viajes por el mundo en Clase Extrema estaban a punto de tocar a su fin. Ya desde la primera noche, unas condiciones durísimas sometieron a los barcos y a los tripulantes a una gran tensión. La aproximación de la flota a Lorient era otro recordatorio más de los desafíos a los que los regatistas modernos se enfrentaban para contener la potencia bruta de los barcos de hoy en día.

Las condiciones y los agotadores océanos habían hecho mella en esta regata, pero fue la implacable competitividad de los propios regatistas lo que de verdad definió la undécima edición de la Volvo Ocean Race. El puro deseo de ganar había convertido ésta, la regata más larga de todas, también en la más exigente física y mentalmente.

Una bulliciosa multitud se acercó al race village de Lorient. Llegaron como devotos de la vela para rendir homenaje al espíritu y al sacrificio de las tripulaciones. Y además, llegaron a animar a sus héroes. Franck Cammas y su equipo se habían propuesto medirse frente a los mejores y, con solo una etapa para terminar, el Groupama 4, estaba perfectamente situado para ganar la Volvo Ocean Race.

La llegada a Galway en cuarto lugar sería suficiente para sellar la victoria. Detrás de ellos, una tremenda batalla se avecinaba entre el PUMA, el CAMPER y el Telefónica. Separados por solo seis puntos, el sueño de la victoria aún estaba vivo pero era la pesadilla de no obtener un puesto en el podio lo que les daba la fuerza. Nunca la distancia entre la gloria y el fracaso fue tan pequeña.

Mientras la afición se dispersaba en Lorient, en Galway comenzaba a congregarse. Ocho meses de mítica navegación culminaban en este momento y la gente de Galway estaba decidida a celebrar a la legendaria manera irlandesa. Poco antes de las 2 de la mañana del 3 de julio, llegó su oportunidad.

中文

16 从阿利坎特一路向南到开普敦的漫漫征程总是充满故事和曲折，这不仅是2011-12沃尔沃环球帆船赛的开局，同时这6500海里的赛段也为整个比赛的发展和结局提供了线索。自从赛事从1997-98赛季改为单一级别赛船以来，凡是赢得第一赛段的船队最终都赢得了整个比赛，这让漫长的第一赛段成为一场至关重要的战役。

在赛前判断获胜的队伍是不可能完成的任务，2011年11月，当各支船队在西班牙白色海岸蓄势待发之际，至少有四支、甚至是五支船队都有可能在高威问鼎最终的荣耀，而以二手船参赛的"三亚号"则不具备挑战领奖台的实力。航海专家唯一能确定的就是，最终的输与赢都在一线之间。

逻辑可以帮我们做判断，但是大自然却不管这一套，第一赛段中极端的状况让之前的预判都统统作废。这个世界体育赛事中最艰苦的赛场充分证明了自然的强大力量，就连一贯以温柔面貌示人的地中海也露出狰狞面目，让若干船队惊心的准备和投入都付之东流。

在陆地上，岸上团队、赛事监控人员、后勤团队和媒体都对这一系列的海上突发事件猝不及防。水手的家人和朋友们都知道，不到船队安全抵达高威的那一天，生活中永远都不会拥有完全的安宁和平静。

刺激和恐惧同时发生，"站在生命之巅"的口号有了全新的注解，对于六十六名水手来说，未来的八个月将是一次引人入胜的极限之旅，对观众而言亦是如此。

38 在赛事五彩斑斓的历史中，各种各样的危险都曾出现过。但是，当2011-12届赛事第一次抵达中东地区时，新的危险又出现了：2011年，东非海域出现的237次海盗袭击让船队前往阿布扎比的路途中出现了极大的危险。

为了确保船队在印度洋的安全，一场史无前例的后勤及运输工程打响了。

作为第八次承担停靠港任务的开普敦和水手们告别后，5430海里的第二赛段打响了，这一赛段被赛事组织者拆分为了两个阶段的比赛。

第一赛段的终点不对外公布，在"隐形区"内，西班牙电信队以微弱的优势战胜看步·新西兰酋长队取得第一阶段的胜利。

在船队到达保密安全港后，船只被载上了全副武装货轮，被一路运送到了阿联酋北部的沙迦港，并从那里开始了一段仅有98海里的冲刺，终点为阿布扎比。

这是一次不允许有任何失误的运输，并向外界发去警告，提示这一海域存在的危险。

52 "欢迎旅者来到阿布扎比"，这句口号因为帆船赛的到来而更加应景。这座城市为沃尔沃环球帆船赛的到来准备了最热情的迎接，2012年1月4日，赛事第一次穿越阿拉伯海域来到阿布扎比，让这里成为赛事环球路线和友谊之旅的重要一站。

几天前，25000名歌迷来到赛事村码头欣赏英国摇滚天团Coldplay的跨年音乐会，正式开启一系列的精彩活动。

沿着阿联酋海岸线的冲刺为当地观众提供了一次近距离观赏顶级帆船赛的机会，超过120000名观众在船队停靠期间来到赛事村，他们为"阿萨姆号"和阿迪尔而来。意味"决心"的"阿萨姆号"终于来到自己的母港，而阿联酋小伙子阿迪尔则承载了这个中东小国巨大的厚望。

对于其他船员，这是一段与家人团聚的幸福时光。第二赛段中支索故障让三亚队缺席阿布扎比，同时也错过了这里港内赛的较量，船队只有等到前往三亚的比赛开始之际才能重返比赛。

68 欢度佳节的人们来到半山半岛码头，然而赛事却是硝烟四起。西班牙电信队无懈可击的表现让其他队伍陷入不利境地，迫使船队需要想办法阻止这支西班牙船队的胜利势头。

比赛至此，已经有四支船队登上过领奖台，但是电信队稳定的发挥让船队的优势越来越明显。不过赛程刚刚过半，还有不少得分的机会，彪马队、看步·新西兰酋长队和安盟保险队的船员深知，第四赛段将是一次比赛的分水岭，此时不发威，更待何时？

与此相反，伊克尔·马丁内兹和队友哈维·费南德斯压力要小得多，在对手焦急应战之时，他们二人共同获得了国际帆联颁发的"年度世界最佳帆船运动员"称号，并且还回到西班牙为奥运会49级双人帆船比赛进行了训练。

南中国海残酷的天气让长达二十天的航行充满艰辛，而第四赛段中最让人印象深刻的是，各支船队抵达奥克兰的时间是如此接近，远洋航海也充满了齐头并进的较量。

84 沃尔沃环球帆船赛诞生于1973年，每届比赛中南大洋的赛段都格外特殊，不少苛刻的航海家把这段险途当作对一名远洋水手的真正考验，穿过和恩角是远洋航海中的一枚荣誉勋章。

当船队驶入浩瀚的太平洋，诸多因素都将影响船队的成绩和发挥。离开温暖的奥克兰，船队将要在6705海里的赛段中经受南纬四十度和五十度的大风大浪，还要接受南美洲合恩角的考验，每只船队都渴望这一赛段冠军能够获得的三十个积分。船队比赛的区域被限制在了南纬58度以北的区域，这样做是为了避免海上浮冰对船只安全造成威胁。

接下来发生的故事则是几家欢乐几家愁了。每一天都有各种事故的报告，每一天都是和狂风大浪肉搏的经历，六支船队中的五支都被迫中途靠岸维修，只有四支船队最终抵达巴西伊塔加。任何一支坚持完成第五赛段的船队都值得赞美，观众们在一边追踪比赛时，也只能一边感叹远洋航海赛之不易。

106 在经过第五赛段扣人心弦的比赛后，水手们终于可以在伊塔加好好修整一番了。在受伤的"三亚号"被货轮运送迈阿密的途中，其他队伍利用伊塔加的宝贵时间修复船只，等待来日再战。

西班牙电信队的连胜已经在一个月前被安盟船员们打破，而现在，彪马队也证明了自己冠军的潜质，不过电信队依然不失为一支强队，在前往迈阿密的最后1500海里的追逐中，彪马和电信事中齐头并进，但最终还是彪马队以微弱优势获胜。

理论上，二十分的领先优势让伊克尔率领的电信队拥有选择战略的自由度，而实际上，强大的对手正在加快追赶的步伐，而电信队却开始不断出现失误。

仅仅17天的时间，赛事格局就发生了如此巨大的变化，这使得2011－12沃尔沃环球帆船赛成为有史以来竞争最激烈的一届赛事，一场鏖战一触即发。

122 2011年11月，本届比赛打响，船队需要环绕地球一周才能抵达终点线。六个月后，船队重新回到伊比利亚半岛，而前四名的船队积分差距依然十分微小。对于这几支船队来说，从迈阿密的启航好像一场新的战役打响。

不像比赛的前半段，船队在此时已经没有太多机会犯错误，他们必须争取每一分，否则就会帮助对手超越自己。对于船长们来说，压力也开始陡增，因为从现在开始，每一场战斗都可能改写积分榜上的排序。

无须赘述，此时没有任何一支船队能够再承受任何失误：从此刻开始，一个小错误就可能导致不可挽回的后果；从此刻开始，所有的船员们都提高了警惕，而船长们背负的压力也陡然提升；从此刻开始，任何得分的机会都绝不能放过。

此时的战局对于西班牙电信队来说可谓乌云密布，而佛罗里达海域的热带风暴阿尔伯托也开始快速形成，这为第七赛段的开局制造了麻烦，也让这场重返欧洲的战役增添了更多可能性。

140 葡萄牙里斯本拥有光辉的航海历史，沃尔沃环球帆船赛的到来为这座伟大的航海城市锦上添花。赛事近四十年的历史中充满着戏剧化的时刻，但是从来没有象本届比赛的这出大戏一样扣人心弦。

第八赛段有很多值得关注的细节，安盟保险队与西班牙电信队的冠军争夺进入白热化，两队的积分差距只有三分，而即将开始的赛段是两队都十分熟悉的海域，想要赢得比赛就不能犯任何错误，否则几年的努力将付之东流，彪马和看步的虎视眈眈以及比斯开湾复杂的天气都让比赛更具看点。

如果只看线路，第八赛段是非常简单的，全长只有1940海里，只需要制定两次战略。但是如果看海上条件的话，情况就要复杂的多了，必须要调动最佳状态和技术才行。

这一赛段是对水手实力的真实考验，在沃尔沃Open70大帆船上，他们将展开牵动人心的激烈竞争。

当船队整装待发时，紧张的气氛充满了里斯本的赛事村，再过不到五天，戏剧将会发展到下一个阶段，让我们久久无法忘怀。

154 一身的疲惫，八个月的航行，极端条件的考验，这一切都将要结束了。从第一夜开始，水手和船只就开始接受严峻的考验，奔向洛里昂的冲刺再一次提醒人们我们这个时代的水手们所面临的挑战。

风暴和骇浪的场景将会成为本届比赛的生动注解，然而真正让第十一届沃尔沃环球帆船赛载入史册的是水手们所展现的伟大的航海精神，这种想要赢得胜利的勇气和决心让比赛成为包含心理和生理双重考验的一场伟大较量。

观众们来到洛里昂赛事村，他们理解航海，他们明白环球水手的付出和坚持，他们也因此将自己毫无保留的欢呼献给法国船长弗兰科·卡玛斯和他的队员们，还剩最后一个赛段，法国安盟保险队已经势在必得。

安盟保险队只要已前四名的身份抵达高威就可以获得总冠军，而彪马队、看步·新西兰酋长队和西班牙电信队仅被六个积分分开，总冠军梦想依然若即若离，而还有一种可能的结局就是被挤下领奖台，天堂和地狱的距离就是这么近。

当洛里昂的人群散去，高威的人们开始汇集，一场伟大的环球航行就要抵达终点，高威的人们要用爱尔兰式的热情庆祝这一时刻的到来。这一刻，锁定在七月三日，凌晨两点。

Credits

Photography

Marc Bow / Volvo Ocean Race
Chris Cameron / CAMPER 2011-12
Nick Dana / Abu Dhabi Ocean Racing / Volvo Ocean Race
Diego Fructuoso / Team Telefónica / Volvo Ocean Race
Hamish Hooper / CAMPER with Emirates Team New Zealand / Volvo Ocean Race
Ronald Koelink
Lagos Sports
Maria Muiña
Yann Riou / Groupama sailing team / Volvo Ocean Race
Ian Roman / Volvo Ocean Race
Amory Ross / PUMA Ocean Racing powered by BERG/ Volvo Ocean Race
Andrés Soriano / Team Sanya / Volvo Ocean Race
Tim Stonton / Volvo Ocean Race
Paul Todd / Volvo Ocean Race
Yvan Zedda / Lorient Grand Large
Yvan Zedda

Image Index